Fabian Bachrach

William Schuman

William Schuman

By

FLORA RHETA SCHREIBER

and

VINCENT PERSICHETTI

G. SCHIRMER, INC.
NEW YORK

COPYRIGHT 1954 BY G. SCHIRMER, INC.

PRINTED IN U.S.A.

The musical examples from the following works are reproduced by permission of the publishers:

Second String Quartet, copyright 1938 by Arrow Music Press, Inc.

This Is Our Time, copyright 1940 by Boosey & Hawkes Inc.

Pioneers! by permission of J. & W. Chester, Ltd., London.

Choral Etude, copyright 1938 by Carl Fischer, Inc. New York.

All of the other examples are copyrighted by G. Schirmer, Inc., as follows: Exx. 2, 9, 26, 32, 45, 117-123—1950; 3, 27, 30, 34, 36, 38, 39-42, 50, 75-90—1942; 6, 8, 12, 13, 14, 20, 22, 23, 29, 33, 37, 47, 49, 91-106—1943; 10, 25—1953; 15—1944; 17-19, 24, 43, 107-116—1946; 21—1945; 44—1952; 46—1940; 48—1939; 53-74—1941.

The title-pages of *Waitin' for the Moon* and *In Love with a Memory of You* are reproduced by permission of Edward B. Marks Music Corporation and Leo Feist, Inc., respectively.

CONTENTS

PAGE

PART ONE: THE MAN *by Flora Rheta Schreiber* 1

PART TWO: THE MUSIC *by Vincent Persichetti* 49

    The Style: Creative Bearings, 49; The Melodic Clue, 51; Harmonic Materials, 58; Rhythmic and Linear Approach, 67; Form Ideas, 71; Orchestral Sense, 74; Vocal Style, 79; New Directions, 84

    American Festival Overture 86

    The Third Symphony 93

    Symphony for Strings 103

    Undertow 108

    Judith 114

APPENDIX

    I. List of Works 126

    II. List of Records 131

    III. Selected List of Articles by William Schuman 133

    IV. Selected Bibliography of Articles on and References to William Schuman . . . 134

INDEX 135

ILLUSTRATIONS

Frontispiece: William Schuman

Between Pages 12 and 13

Schuman at the age of 14
Schuman with his father, mother, and sister, 1931
Title-pages of two popular songs by Schuman
Schuman with his class at Sarah Lawrence College, 1940

Between Pages 28 and 29

Schuman, 1943
Schuman and Koussevitzky, 1944
William and Frances Schuman, 1944
Martha Graham as Judith, 1951

Between Pages 44 and 45

Schuman with Barber, Copland, Thomson, and Menotti, 1952
A page from the autograph manuscript of Schuman's Violin Concerto

Between Pages 60 and 61

Schuman at a UNESCO meeting. Third from left, Malipiero; to Schuman's left, Honegger, Ibert, and Egge
Schuman with his wife and children, Anthony and Andrea

Part One

THE MAN

I

IN THE HOUSEHOLD of Samuel and Ray Schuman in New York City on the morning of August 4, 1910, the family's second child was born. They called him William Howard after William Howard Taft.

William Howard was one day to make a place for himself in the world of music, but the only trace of music in his family is to be found in his paternal grandfather, who was an amateur flute-player, the son of the jeweler to Ludwig II of Bavaria.

The jeweler's son had run away from his native Munich in his teens and had sailed to America. No sooner had he landed in New Orleans than he was drafted into military service with the Confederate Army. Shortly after the War he settled in New Jersey. His wife, who was self-taught, would often quote to her children from Goethe and Schiller, and the composer still remembers the sound of her dramatic recitations. In her eighties Rosa Schuhmann was still vigorously part of the life of the family.

Grandpa Heilbrunn, a hearty peasant from a village near Eisenach, the birthplace of Bach, began working in the New York stockyards as a boy of fifteen. He later became a dealer in cattle and still later dealt in farm real estate. An extremely practical person, he had a strict slogan for the good life: "Every man must have a trade." But he had his lighter side, too, and mostly it was Bill who evoked it. He introduced his grandson to Harry Lauder records on a new disk victrola. When the child got to know all the songs,

Grandpa took him to a vaudeville show to hear Lauder in person. Four-year-old Bill just stood up and sang along. Grandpa saw nothing wrong in his grandson's singing out boldly. The child kept going. Lauder stopped and let him go on alone. Anyway, that's how Grandpa told the story.

Bill was full of mischief. Later on, when he was fourteen, he decided in characteristically businesslike fashion that something should be done to make adults aware of children's real wishes. He began keeping a notebook of what he would like to have parents do. That was so he could use it as a reference book when he was forty and a parent. Mischief, however, did not keep him from being one of the top six in his class or from being transferred from Manhattan's P.S. 165 to Speyer Experimental Junior High School for Boys on West 126th Street, a school for students of superior intelligence.

While Bill was still in grade school, he began to show evidence of a flair for organization. At this time he organized an athletic club. During his high-school days, he formed the Milray Outing Club, which was surely the first Baby Sitters' League. Parents paid a tuition fee of fifteen dollars per month so that, between 3:30 p.m. and 5:30 p.m. on week days and all day on Saturday, their children could box, wrestle, run, and, of course, play baseball under Bill's watchful eye. Bill was an able teacher in the rudiments of these sports. And so he could supplement his very adequate allowance with additional spending money. The desire for spending money always stimulated his ingenuity. If he wanted something, he usually found the way to get it.

If the boys on his block (West 112th Street in his highschool days) enticed him into the streets, the family exerted a counter-pull, drawing him back home. Home was a comfortable place. The family was not rich but never poor, and by the time Bill was in his teens his father had risen from a bookkeeper to vice-president of the large printing firm of Oberly and Newell. Both parents were born in New York City of German-Jewish descent. The two dominant influences in their household were a strong sense of ethics and an enthusiastic Americanism. Samuel Schuman[1] had served in the Spanish-American War, was active as a Spanish-American War veteran, was proud of his Americanism, and used to instill this pride in his children. He would fill them with a vision of their country that combined the practicality of the Chamber of Commerce with the rapture of Walt Whitman.

Home was filled with a strong sentimentality and a strong cohesiveness. Of a Sunday night the clan would gather, singing Victor Herbert scores and light operas of the day. Cousin Ruth Wertheim would be at the piano, mother and sister Audrey would sing. Bill would sing or play the violin or do both. Father would sometimes join in, but more often he preferred listening from his comfortable chair. When the family itself was silent, Caruso would raise his voice on the phonograph. Such activities did not indicate a special bent towards music; they simply represented one of the ways in which an average middle-class family amused itself in those pre-radio times.

Bill played the violin at these family sessions without having any serious musical interest. He had asked to have lessons but took them reluctantly, as most children do. Blanche Schwarz, his violin teacher, used to lure him from the streets for his lesson and Mrs. Schuman would stand at the door warning, "I'm afraid I'll have to stop Billy's lessons if he doesn't practice." Billy wouldn't be listening . . . his thoughts would still be with baseball.

One Friday evening the pupils of Blanche Schwarz showed their musical mettle at Wurlitzer Auditorium. Bill, now fourteen, played MacDowell's *To a Wild Rose* and a Serenade by Pierné. His sister accompanied him on the piano. He also was one of a quartet playing Handel's Largo. The next year's concert was at Chickering Hall for the benefit of the Godmother's League. This time Bill played Borowski's *Adoration*, Kéler-Béla's *Son of Puszta*, and Daula's *Carnival of Venice*.

---

[1] Who adopted the simplified spelling of the family name.

School work held no more fascination for Bill than did the violin. At Speyer Junior High School, his real interest was the theater. He was voted the best orator, and the school's yearbook, *The Credonian*, stated that his ambition was to be a theatrical producer. A play written by him was performed at Speyer. It was called *College Chums* and had a serious, didactic purpose. There were two main characters—a studious boy and a baseball player. Each rejected the other but in the end each was won over to the other's side. The youthful playwright argued that moderation should be the goal for everyone. It was the last time he was to uphold such a philosophy.

In 1925 Bill was selected as one of a group of school boys to spend a summer in France under the auspices of the French Government. It was his first trip abroad, and with it came a feeling of independence, a quickening. When he came home he was graduated from Speyer to George Washington High School. One tangible result of the feeling of independence was the formation of a jazz band. The band rehearsed in the living room of the Schuman home and in time performed at dances. His sister secured its first important engagement at Hunter College, where she was a student. Hunter decided that the band was a lively one and many engagements followed. Bill performed several functions: not only was he founder and business manager but he also played the fiddle and the banjo, besides appearing as vocal soloist. After a fashion, quite sketchy and quite his own, he could "play" every instrument in the band, conduct and do some arranging, a wholly unorthodox kind of arranging. He would teach the instrumentalists their parts by rote. There was no other way, since he was unschooled in the writing of a score. At a contest of New York City high school orchestras, he played the double-bass part of the *Oberon Overture*. Most of the competing orchestras were short of bass players and Bill was drafted into group after group. His parents sat through twelve performances of the Overture and liked it.

The jazz band thrived. Its leader's quick grasp of essentials led him to take his studies lightly; he was indifferent even to a music course in scales and notation, but was nevertheless a good student. In everything except drawing. His drawing was so bad that he failed the same course over and over again and it looked as though he would not graduate. He went to the principal and expostulated on the weakness of an educational system so rigid that it demanded the impossible of its students. He won the argument and graduation.

Except for the summer in France, his summers from the time he was eleven until he was out of his teens were spent at Camp Cobbossee in Maine. He was highly proficient in all camp activities and was popular with the campers. At Cobbossee there took place the première of the very first Schuman work. It was a violin tango called *Fate*. The composer was little more than sixteen and still preferred baseball to music.

Schuman's collaborator in many an early musical venture was Edward B. Marks, Jr.[1] Bill and Eddie were inseparable friends from the time they were thirteen until they were twenty-one. Together they put on a minstrel show, Marks writing the lyrics and Schuman the music. As the years went on, songs were forever singing their way into Bill's consciousness and he began feeble attempts to put the melodic lines down on paper. During the last five years of this period, he wrote a total of some one hundred songs, many of them composed for special occasions.

Schuman sometimes wrote his own words, more often the words came from Marks. Their collaboration culminated in a musical comedy called *It's Up to Pa*, which was performed with great success by the campers under the direction of Anthony Ross.[2] Two of the tunes from the show were published.

---

[1] Later an executive in various government and international social agencies.

[2] Ross later became an actor. He has appeared on Broadway in *The Glass Menagerie*, *Arsenic and Old Lace*, *Season in the Sun*, and other plays.

Getting songs written was becoming a preoccupation. He wrote songs for popular music publishers, prepared night club material, and drummed up business for new tunes in a nightly beat of dance halls and clubs. He collaborated with a childhood friend, Frank Loesser,[1] in writing songs. Usually, as in the case of Loesser's first published song—*In Love with a Memory of You*—, the music was Schuman's, the words Loesser's. They turned out some forty popular songs, but the team's only success lay in the occasional sale of special material written for vaudeville and night-club entertainers. Schuman has since boasted playfully that he is alone in having the distinction of writing an unsuccessful song with Frank Loesser. If Schuman had held on, he might have become a Tin Pan Alley success. But in the back of his mind was a growing suspicion that he didn't really know what he was doing, that perhaps he was not "chording" his melodies satisfactorily. There was a hankering to know how, yet the hankering somehow remained vague and repressed. Other boys were going into business and, since he didn't have anything he particularly wanted to do, he registered, after graduation from George Washington High School in February 1928, at the New York University School of Commerce.

In this period, Schuman in his derby, strutting with a sense of his onrushing manhood and expanding masculine ego, was markedly under the influence of the times, of what has been called the roaring twenties, and he was virtually a character out of the pages of F. Scott Fitzgerald. There were the practical jokes, the bull sessions in a rented furnished apartment in Greenwich Village, the meetings of the UMPPA (United Musical Poker Players

---

[1] Loesser became one of the most successful popular-song writers in the country. His long string of hits include such songs—for which he wrote both words and music—as *Baby, It's Cold Outside, On a Slow Boat to China,* and *Praise the Lord and Pass the Ammunition,* as well as the complete scores for the musicals *Where's Charley?* and *Guys and Dolls* and the movie *Hans Christian Andersen.*

of America), an improvised party that Bill gave as a nonpaying guest of a New York hotel.

Outwardly aggressive, with the reputation of being a wild boy, he was also sensitive and conservative. Though he knew many girls, his relationships with them tended to be consecutive rather than simultaneous. He instinctively chose a one-woman family-man pattern of existence. One thing he mentioned to nobody was his love of poetry. He regarded this love as his soft side, a side he didn't care to show. But canoeing at Cobbossee was for him not just sport. It was a chance to get off alone and read the poets, particularly the Romantics, until his eyes grew blurred through the combined effects of sun and sentiment.

Some months before his twentieth birthday there came a moment seemingly unrelated to all that had gone before, a moment that was to stand out vividly as the climax of his youth. His sister had an extra ticket to the New York Philharmonic and with the help of her mother finally persuaded him to go to the concert. He had never heard a concert of serious music and felt certain that he would be bored.

It was April 4, 1930. The Philharmonic's program consisted of Robert Schumann's Symphony No. 3, the funeral music from *Götterdämmerung,* and *Summer Evening* by Kodály. The details of the program meant little to Schuman. For him the concert held a private meaning. He felt as if his head would split with the surge of impressions, as if his heart would snap with sheer excitement. Particularly exciting were the way all the fiddlers bowed together and the force with which they could attack a chord. He was intrigued by the tunes that changed as they recurred and the measures in which the drummer had nothing to play. There seemed to be more inventive ability displayed at this one concert by the New York Philharmonic than by all the jazz bands on Broadway. The evening meant discovery. It was poignant, pregnant of things to come, and baffling.

The next day Schuman returned to school as usual, but he could not forget the sound of a hundred instruments, a sound that made his professor's voice seem like the distant whistle of a departing train. He caught the drift of the lecture: "A man in business needs a cool, keen, sober imagination." It was too much. Young Schuman's fevered brain could not endure the use of the word "imagination" in this context. At the end of the hour, he left the lecture hall and walked quickly out of the building, moving through Washington Square, walking fast, knowing that he was leaving the New York University School of Commerce behind him. He went back, collected the unexpired balance of his tuition fee, and went on walking. He also made a 'phone call to the Paramount Advertising Agency to say he was quitting. He had spent his spare time at the agency doing copy work for a candy account and learning the lingo. And so he walked the streets. He fully realized the odds against his setting out to study music seriously. But what had been vague and repressed when he entered the School of Commerce was now clear and compelling. He knew music was what he wanted.

His eye caught a sign: Malkin Conservatory. He found himself in the lobby of a private house and registered for a course in harmony because he had heard somewhere that composers begin by studying harmony.

Schuman's family knew that he hadn't found himself yet and was therefore prepared to have him change his direction. They had tried to let him find his own way with the assurance that he had both economic and emotional support from them. But this decision, unrelated to any interest he had ever shown, was something else. "Bill", his father said that evening, "you don't have to be a business man if you don't want to, but if you go into music, you're up against genius. If you're not at the top, it's no good."

The parents sat quietly when Bill left the room. He seemed to think there was nothing especially dramatic about his decision but they were worried. His father kept saying: "He is almost twenty. Even if he has talent, it is so late to begin. Even if he has it, and how do we know that he has? Where has it been hiding itself all these years? All that jazz doesn't mean a thing. This is entirely different. Why should I let him make a failure of himself when he has everything in him that could make for success?" But Schuman's mind was made up and there was nothing the parents could do but hope for the best and give him every possible encouragement.

Max Persin was the harmony teacher at the Malkin Conservatory. It was the merest accident that it was he rather than another, another who would teach from a textbook of dull orthodoxy. The teacher would say: "Let's look at music and find what makes it tick, what causes one composer to sound different from another. The mystery is the genius, but there is no mystery about the manipulation of materials." The teacher was acutely aware of trends in new music and a contemporary work would be given a thorough technical and esthetic analysis. "I promised him nothing", Persin said years later, "but I could see there was something burning there." Schuman would listen avidly. The little man with the European manner, with a spirit of ancient wisdom combined with an acute awareness of the present, living quietly in a Bronx tenement with a sister who considered him a prophet, became a prophet to the student, too. They would spend four or five hours together, listening to symphonies. Schuman would grow hungry and amidst all the revelation would be realistic enough to wonder whether the teacher ever ate.

From harmony with Persin, Schuman went on to counterpoint with Charles Haubiel. The new teacher called him "William" and William was quiet, polite, and acquiescent during the year in which he learned his counterpoint. He worked at it from eight to ten hours a day and by the end of the year was writing exercises in 14 parts. While studying with Persin and then Haubiel, Schuman composed popular songs, made arrangements for jazz bands,[1] and even did some song-plugging. He also took a part-time job at Oberly and Newell's, his father's printing business, and tried many side ventures. One of these was the Wilfred Publishing Company, which he organized with Ferdinand Nauheim.[2] The firm was on the lookout for unpublished writers interested in publishing their work on a cooperative basis but, though there were plenty of willing writers, the high-minded partners lost money and ultimately discontinued their business.

Schuman began to find these side ventures, his father's printing business, and particularly Tin Pan Alley uncongenial ways of making a living. He decided to teach music because teaching would give him the opportunity to do a creative job and to be his own patron. In 1933 he became a freshman at Teachers College, Columbia University. He wasn't happy there: he felt uneasy in an atmosphere where emphasis was placed on how to teach music rather than on the music taught. He deplored Teachers College's approach to musical education, though he had a high regard for some of the members of the faculty. Some of his interest in educational reform stems from these days.

During his college years he continued to compose. His dislike of Tin Pan Alley increased. For a while he toyed with compromises. He considered spending six months with jazz and six months with serious music. He began to compose an operetta, with a libretto by Loesser, on the life of Leonardo da Vinci. He finally realized that as long as he was exposed to Broadway's banalities, he would naturally be obliged to write down to commercial standards. He found the conservative and tradition-ridden

---

[1] Schuman taught himself how to do this by writing out the parts (not a score) of an arrangement of a popular song, cajoling the players in a dance hall on 59th Street (by giving them cigarettes) to try out the parts, and then making the necessary changes as they played.

[2] An author and advertising consultant.

policies of Broadway more and more distasteful and knew that the umbilical cord that united him with commercial music had to be cut. Nevertheless as late as 1934, he wrote both words and music for a musical comedy called *Fair Enough,* which was produced at Brant Lake Camp, where he was a counsellor. The show's *Adirondack Air* became a local hit, but its composer was no longer interested. The umbilical cord had been cut.

Schuman received his Bachelor of Science degree in 1935 after two years of study and he began looking for a job as a teacher. He didn't want to be a hack teacher, enunciating dead dicta to minds made unreceptive through self-protection against boredom. But he did want to teach. Since the College placement bureau was not helpful, he decided to help himself. In the spring of the year he went to the desk at the Teachers' College Library and asked for catalogues of schools within a twenty-mile radius of New York City. But, as he turned the pages of unrewarding catalogue after unrewarding catalogue, his mind swam in a morass of conventionality and prim academic orthodoxy. In one catalogue, however,—that of Sarah Lawrence College—his eye caught phrases that echoed his own beliefs: "In a very real sense, all education is self-education, but some environments are more favorable to the process than others." He called Sarah Lawrence on the 'phone. Its voice was cool, professional, candid. There were no openings. "But", he replied as if he were stating an indisputable fact, "if what you print in your catalogue is true, your president should be glad to see me." An appointment was made for six weeks later.

Constance Warren, the president of the college, was pleased with his enthusiasm but had no job to give him. She suggested that the voice teacher, Jerome Swinford, a member of the Faculty Advisory Committee on Appointments, might be of some help. Through Swinford, Schuman met Horace Grenell, another member of the faculty. Grenell arranged an audition for Schuman with the Brooklyn Ethical Culture School, where there was an opening for a music teacher. Schuman worked late into the night preparing to conduct a Haydn symphony, only to face different music in the morning. He found he had to conduct a rhythm band of eight-to-ten-year-olds playing compositions written especially for them and he had to lead the school assembly in singing *Scotland's Burning, Fire, Fire.* The principal closed the door on him with a polite but perverse "Male teachers are not good for a school of this kind. The children try to imitate the man's voice and sing an octave lower."

Schuman tried Sarah Lawrence again. Some months had gone by and in the interval the college had received a grant from the Rockefeller Foundation for exploratory courses for freshmen in various fields including the arts. Miss Warren thought that Schuman might be worked into the new program. Almost instinctively he viewed it with an administrator's eye. "But, Miss Warren," he pointed out, "the course will lack unity and coherence if the men from the different fields are picked at random. On the other hand no one except a Da Vinci could represent all fields. May I suggest that one man act as coordinator, working from a single focal point, and find others on the faculty to work with him on the project?" He appeared before the elected Faculty Advisory Committee on Appointments. The tribunal posed its first question: "Mr. Schuman, exactly what is your idea of an educated person?" "I can best give my definition by stating what education is not", Schuman began. His definition amounted to a diatribe against education based on *a priori* judgments and rigid procedures. "Education", he said, "must be a continuing process, leading to no musical coda upon graduation, but continuing all through life." "Mr. Schuman, to which esthetic theories do you subscribe?" His reply, in which he championed some of John Dewey's premises as expressed in *Art As Experience,* impressed the committee. In September he became the one man he had previously suggested to Miss Warren.

Now that he had a job for the fall, he could allow

Schuman at the age of 14

Schuman with his father, mother, and sister, 1931

Title-pages of two popular songs by Schuman

Fritz Henle

Schuman with his class at Sarah Lawrence
College, 1940

his thoughts to dwell on Frances Prince, whom he had loved for almost four years. Frances came from the same kind of family as his; they had met when he was twenty-one and she was eighteen. It was at the time when he was secretly trying to ween himself away from popular music and she found him a little remote, preoccupied. But in time, the dam of his reticence unlocked itself and he told her that he had recently made a very important decision, that he felt he was becoming a new and quite different person, that, above everything on earth, he wanted to be a composer of serious music. He told her: "I started late. Very late. I have to make up for lost time."

Frances Prince was in every way sympathetic to his musical ambitions. When he wanted to take violin lessons again, but felt he ought not to spend the money, they worked out a three-cornered arrangement—Schuman taught Miss Prince counterpoint; in return she taught Miss Schwarz, his old violin teacher, Italian; and in return for that Schuman got his violin lessons from Miss Schwarz. Schuman wanted to hear as much music as possible, so they went to concerts very frequently. They always sat apart so that he would be free to concentrate and, score in hand, could soak in the symphonic repertory in a race to make up for all the lost concerts. He "won" what was purported to be a scholarship in conducting at the Mozarteum in Salzburg. Later he discovered that he would have to pay for this "scholarship". He decided to go anyway. Salzburg was away from Frances, but by now she knew that his return would eventually lead to their marriage.

II

IN SEPTEMBER 1935 William Schuman returned to New York from a summer in Salzburg—a twenty-five-year-old musical nonentity. He was apprehensive as he approached New York Harbor, apprehensive and driven by a powerfully propelling trinity of wishes—to succeed in his new job at Sarah Lawrence College, to marry Frances Prince, to find himself as a composer.

At the Mozarteum Academy in Salzburg he had done enough work in conducting to earn his certificate, but only just enough. The greater part of his time was spent working on a symphony. The first ideas had come while he was in Paris, and in Paris, too, most of his time was spent composing. The germ of the symphony was his own *Choreographic Poem,* written for a small group of instrumentalists a few years earlier.

On March 27, 1936, during his first year at Sarah Lawrence, Schuman married Frances Prince. He then submitted his symphony for the Bearns Prize at Columbia University. The previous year he had entered *Chorale Canons.*[1] The Canons had not won a prize but had won enthusiastic comment from Daniel Gregory Mason, chairman of the Music Department at Columbia University and director of the contest. Now, however, Dr. Mason failed to respond to the symphony; it seemed to him a

---

[1] The *Chorale Canons* (later published under the title of Four Canonic Choruses), consist of *Epitaph* with words by Edna St. Vincent Millay; *Epitaph for Joseph Conrad* by Countee Cullen; *Night Stuff* by Carl Sandburg; and *Come not* by Tennyson.

conscious attempt to register with the modernists. Schuman, who had no predisposition towards either the conservatives or the modernists, believed that the professor was discouraging him from finding his own idiom simply and naturally, only because that idiom seemed to be in disharmony with the professor's own musical philosophy. The Bearns rejection was disillusioning and disillusionment persisted until the summer of 1936, when Schuman sought out Roy Harris at the Juilliard School of Music.

Harris read the score of Symphony No. I with surgeonlike scrutiny and found it weak. Yet he knew there was one good thing about it—that the intensity with which the composer wanted it to be good was good, that so fierce had been the desire to write a symphony that a symphony had to be written. Harris admitted Schuman to three courses and saw that the problem was to release him, to show him that a composer's world could not be finite, that it must be fluid.

At the end of his first summer with Harris at Juilliard, Schuman earned three A-plusses. This was an auspicious beginning of a teacher-pupil relationship that was to last for two years. Autumn found Schuman again studying with Harris, now privately, and becoming the faithful disciple. The lessons in Harris's Princeton home were long, concentrated studies in compositional material. Through Harris, Schuman became interested in early music, in medieval modes. In his own works Harris had applied the principles of this early music and he now explained the principles to Schuman. In Harris's early works Schuman heard sounds he had never before heard in music and the influence was strong. So, too, was the influence of Harris's ideas on polyharmony.

The First Symphony was performed at a Composers' Forum Laboratory concert of the Works Progress Administration in the fall of 1936. Jules Werner conducted and Harris was present. On hearing the work, Schuman realized what Harris had meant when he had said that the symphony was long on thematic material, short on development. The First String Quartet and the Canonic Choruses were also performed on the same program. The Quartet, like Symphony No. I, was a fiasco. Not so the Choruses, conducted by Lehman Engel. The audience was highly responsive.

It was the period of the Spanish Civil War and that war was extending its long arm into American cultural life. The Musicians' Committee of the North American Committee to Aid Spanish Democracy held a contest, with Bernard Wagenaar, Roger Sessions, Aaron Copland, and Roy Harris as judges. The prize was to include performance, publication, and recording of the winning work. Schuman had by now completed his Symphony No. II, and it won the contest. But, because the sponsoring group had failed to raise the necessary funds, the prize did not bring the promised performance, publication, or recording. The prize did have one very important practical effect: it brought the work of William Schuman to the attention of Aaron Copland. The two men had met socially but Copland had regarded Schuman merely as an engaging young man, who taught music at Sarah Lawrence. Now Copland began to watch Schuman's career. In the May-June 1938 issue of *Modern Music* Copland wrote:

Schuman is, so far as I am concerned, the musical find of the year. There is nothing puny or miniature about this young man's talent. If he fails he will fail on a grand scale. His eight-part chorus *Pioneers* . . . tries characteristically for big things. It is carefully planned music—music of design rather than melodic inspiration. When the planning is too evident, as it sometimes is, the effect is unspontaneous. But for the most part, this is music of tension and power—a worthy match for Walt Whitman's stirring text. From this piece alone, it seems to me that Schuman is a composer who is going places.

Thirteen years later, in the July 1951 issue of *The Musical Quarterly,* Copland was to write: "A composition like the Fourth String Quartet makes one understand why Schuman is generally ranked among the top men of American music." And once again Copland was to prophesy, for in the quartet he was to find a new quality "that presages an enlargement of the capacities of the William Schuman we already know".

In this same article Copland was to comment on Schuman's rhythms—on "those curiously Schumanesque rhythms, so skittish and personal, so utterly free and inventive". Copland was to go so far as to say: "There is nothing quite like these rhythms in American music, or any music for that matter."

The same month (June 1938) that Copland's earlier article appeared, Copland himself heard Schuman's Symphony No. II under the baton of Edgar Schenkman conducting the WPA's Greenwich Village Orchestra. When the Columbia Broadcasting System presented the symphony with Howard Barlow conducting, Copland listened again. He spoke to Serge Koussevitzky. In February (1939) Koussevitzky conducted the symphony in Boston.

Schuman went to Boston for a week of rehearsals, a tumultuous week. There was anxiety engendered by the hostile response to the radio broadcast of the symphony. There was also confidence inspired by the fact that a Harvard student named Leonard Bernstein, generally considered Harvard's bright boy of music, had asked to see the score, and reading it, had derived much from it. There were the gaucheries of being a novice, of arriving at Symphony Hall at eight a.m. when the rehearsal had not been called until ten, of being challenged for hanging around the stage door. But there was also the experience of observing Serge Koussevitzky, magnificent in fur hat and fur-lined coat, enter the stage door of Symphony Hall and come to a full stop before him, saying with a sweeping gesture of inclusion: "Ah, the composer!" There was the silent frigidity with which most of the audience greeted the symphony, the few hisses, and at the end the audience's smug retreat from the music of that awful William Schuman. But backstage there was compensation. Koussevitzky had predicted: "This will not be a success with the public, but with me it is a success and you must hear." Now that Schuman had heard, he made a serious avowal: he promised the conductor a new work in a short time. A few minutes after that the Schumans were safe at a movie, succumbing to the excitements of a Western. But with morning there was no escape. There was the awakening to reviews repudiating the symphony as ugly, as meaning obscured by the artist's own shadow, as a violent assault on the sensibilities. Moses Smith, the critic of the Boston Transcript, was alone in raising a favorable voice. Smith wrote: ". . . Dr. Koussevitzky, far from having made a mistake in placing it on one of his programs, is actually disclosing to Boston audiences a genuine American talent."

Another strong, positive note was struck by Paul Rosenfeld in the July 1939 issue of *The Musical Quarterly*. The fact that Rosenfeld discussed Schuman in the same article with Copland and Harris was in itself a tribute. And Rosenfeld was explicit in his praise. He described Schuman's Symphony No. II and *Prologue* for chorus and orchestra as "exceptional new American compositions". Rosenfeld also wrote enthusiastically of Schuman's "very shapely Second String Quartet" (1937).

The fact that many in Boston regarded Schuman's Second Symphony as the most disliked work they had ever heard their orchestra play did not daunt him; he began at once to think about the new work he had promised Koussevitzky. He was determined to get a hearing in the festival of American music to be held early in the fall of 1939 under the auspices of the American Society of Composers, Authors and Publishers.

Roy Harris was helping Koussevitzky with the arrangements for the festival. Schuman persuaded Harris to let him submit an overture on speculation. To work on the new overture, which he called *American Festival Overture* in honor of the occasion for which it was written, Schuman retreated to the home of Amy and

Walter Charak in Martha's Vineyard.[1] As soon as the work took shape Schuman hastened to Princeton for Harris's verdict. While Harris shaved, Schuman sang him the fugue theme. "Swell", said Harris. This was the first time Harris had unreservedly approved a Schuman musical concept at first hearing.

Koussevitzky included the overture in the festival. After a rehearsal the conductor asked for Schuman's opinion of the work. "The ending is wrong", Schuman replied. The conductor whispered: "Sh-h—you and I are the the only people who know that." There was no time to change the ending and the conductor was right about no one's noticing it anyway. At the Boston première (Oct. 6, 1939) the overture was a success with conductor and audience alike. "Fine!" said Koussevitzky. "Now you must begin to hate Roy Harris." Schuman knew that this was Koussevitzky's way of saying that he had come of age musically. Schuman's first act under the new order was to rewrite the ending of the overture for the New York première.

February 27, 1940, saw the first performance of String Quartet No. III, written on commission from Town Hall and the League of Composers, the first commission awarded jointly by these organizations. The Coolidge Quartet performed this work at a Town Hall concert. Olin Downes found energy and assurance in the part-writing but was unable to predict whether this energy and assurance were more than part of an experimental phase. Irving Kolodin in the New York Sun dismissed the work as inferior to Schuman's *Prologue*, performed the previous spring.

On July 4, 1940, an audience at the Lewisohn Stadium responded warmly to *This Is Our Time*, a "secular cantata" with a text by Genevieve Taggard. Alexander Smallens[2] conducted the People's Philharmonic Chorus,

---

[1] Amy Charak is Frances Schuman's aunt.
[2] On July 15, 1942, Smallens conducted another Schuman Stadium première, the orchestral version of *Newsreel*.

19

made up of iron workers, painters, carpenters, workers in shoe factories, housewives, and white-collar workers. "Workers sing the way Valkyries ought to", wrote Henry Simon in PM. Schuman had first heard the chorus in a broadcast from the World's Fair and brought it to Smallens's attention. In a New York Times Sunday article, Schuman wrote: "Music which the layman can perform is essential if we hope to reach a wide audience."

The year 1941 was a climactic one. On October 17 Koussevitzky conducted Symphony No. III in Boston. The once hostile Boston critics were friendly. The critic of the Boston Herald was not content merely to praise the new symphony. He had found nothing but ugliness in the Second, but now he reconsidered. "Doubtless", he wrote, "we should now hear in it many virtues which were obtusely hidden from us at that time." From Roy Harris came congratulations; from Olin Downes, for the New York performance (Nov. 22), an accolade. "It is a symphony", Downes wrote, "which for this chronicler takes the position of the best work by an American of the rising generation." "Young Mr. Schuman", as the critics were fond of calling him, was hailed in the December 6 *New Yorker* magazine as "the composer of the hour by virtue of the popular and critical success of his Third Symphony". New York's one-year-old Music Critics' Circle presented its first award, for the best orchestral work of the season, to Schuman's Symphony No. III.

The Fourth Symphony, completed a few months after the Third, was first performed by Arthur Rodzinski[1] with the Cleveland Orchestra (January 22, 1942). Philadelphia and New York performances under the baton of Eugene Ormandy followed. Schuman was filled with a new confidence in the ability of his music to make its way if it was heard. He was therefore unprepared for the turn in his critical fortunes. Downes found the symphony

---

[1] Rodzinski later conducted another Schuman première, that of the *William Billings Overture*, with the New York Philharmonic-Symphony Orchestra (Feb. 17, 1944).

"disappointing", Virgil Thomson pointed a censorious finger and wrote: "He reminds me of Theodore Dreiser. I should like to put him to work writing incidental music for plays or doing ballet scores. I fancy the necessity of making music say something briefly and clearly and simply would be a valuable experience for him."

On January 13, 1943, Town Hall presented a program entirely devoted to Schuman's music. The composer had wanted to include some choral pieces and had cast about for a group that would perform them. Someone told him about a brilliant young conductor who worked for Fred Waring but had also organized his own chorus. Schuman heard the group and had it engaged for his concert, which was regarded by the press as marking the début of Robert Shaw and the Collegiate Chorale. On the same program Rosalyn Tureck and the Saidenberg Sinfonietta gave the first performance of Schuman's Concerto for Piano and Orchestra.

When Schuman completed a new symphony for the Koussevitzky Music Foundation, that symphony (first performed by the Boston Symphony on November 12, 1943) was his fifth. But he could not bring himself to call it that and settled on Symphony for Strings. The New York Times found the new symphony "dry and not particularly communicative" but the Boston critics were ungrudging in their praise. The Boston Daily Globe believed that Schuman was now moving towards a unique personal idiom and the Boston Herald went so far as to say that he was "well on his way to becoming the foremost American-born composer of the day".

Virgil Thomson had repeatedly insisted that Schuman's talent lay in the theater. In 1945 Schuman had the opportunity to try his hand at this genre. The choreographer Antony Tudor asked him to do a ballet score. The collaboration was mostly a long-distance affair, with Tudor on the West Coast and Schuman in New York. The result was *Undertow*. The first performance by the Ballet Theatre at the Metropolitan Opera House on

April 10, 1945, was well received by the dance world; the work was described by *Newsweek* as a "Sex Murder on Toes". It was first performed—with success—as a concert piece by the Los Angeles Philharmonic Orchestra conducted by Alfred Wallenstein; but in New York this version was dismissed coolly at first, except by Virgil Thomson. Thomson believed Schuman's true talent was fulfilling itself.

Another venture connected with the theater was *Side Show*, an orchestral piece written for Billy Rose's revue, *The Seven Lively Arts*. On January 7, 1945, Fritz Reiner conducted the symphonic-orchestra version of *Side Show*[1] with the Pittsburgh Symphony Orchestra. The title was later changed to *Circus Overture*.

* * *

It was natural that Schuman's theatrical flair should some day find expression in opera. And it was natural that the baseball-loving Schuman should choose for his first opera a baseball theme. And so, in 1953, he completed *The Mighty Casey*. On May 4 of that year the opera, with a libretto by Jeremy Gury, had its world première in the Burns Auditorium of the Hartt Music School in Hartford.[2]

The New York Herald Tribune commented editorially: Since Casey's story is as tragic as any in all literature, it is surprising that no one has previously transformed it into opera, an art form which revels in misfortunes . . . Previous operas have dealt with soldiers and lovers, demons and clowns, and surely there is a touch of each in Casey, the heroic figure who goes down swinging as well as singing. At any rate, the Professor's [i.e. Schuman's] outfield opus seems to have won the approval of the discerning fans who were at the opener. So enthusiastic were they that one is tempted to suggest that the work be exported. Italy once sent us *The Girl of the Golden West*. Perhaps we can reciprocate with *Cassio al Bastone*.

---

[1] Maurice Abravanel had conducted the small-orchestra version of *Side Show* on December 17, 1944, in Philadelphia.

[2] Gury is a vice-president of the advertising agency, Benton and Bowles.

In a less facetious vein Arthur Berger (New York Herald Tribune, May 5, 1953) wrote: "The harmonies are, for my taste, too colored, at times, for the simplicity, and appropriate simplicity, of the melodies. But Schuman is very, very expert, indeed, in his technical handling, his orchestration and his general ease."

All through the years of Schuman's early career as a composer, he continued to build a separate career at Sarah Lawrence College, where at first he had been the energetic amateur, rushing in where traditionalists feared to tread. His students found him stimulating and original and made him their confidant.

Schuman became conductor of the Sarah Lawrence chorus in 1938 after the chorus had struggled for a number of years valiantly but vainly. He persuaded the chorus to commission composers to write new works; he arranged for joint concerts with choruses from Yale, Harvard, and Williams; he organized a symposium for performance and discussion of student compositions of college music groups from Bennington, Vassar, Princeton, and Sarah Lawrence itself. When the chorus went on tour, the college followed. *The Campus,* the school newspaper, wrote: "Our chorus is the football team of Sarah Lawrence. Notre Dame had Knute, but we have Bill." The high point of the chorus's career was its performance, on February 14, 1943, of Debussy's *La Damoiselle Elue* with the Boston Symphony, conducted by Koussevitzky, in Carnegie Hall.

Schuman wrote both band and choral works which were performed by college groups throughout the country. The band of Pennsylvania State College gave the first performance of his *Newsreel In Five Shots* (1942). In March 1943 the Harvard Glee Club, the Radcliffe Choral Society, and the Boston Symphony Orchestra, conducted by Koussevitzky, gave the first performance of *A Free Song,* Secular Cantata No. II, with words by Walt Whitman. Schuman himself conducted his own chorus in his *Prelude for Voices* with words by Thomas Wolfe (1940) and, together with the Harvard Glee Club, *Te Deum* (1945). This last work and a song for voice and piano, *Orpheus with his Lute*, were remnants of incidental music Schuman composed for a production of *Henry VIII* that was planned by Margaret Webster.

Over a beer with Norman Lloyd, another music instructor at the college, Schuman used to yield to dreamy illusion-spinning. At such moments, he would sharply criticize most music education and especially the teaching of music theory. He would theorize grandiosely about what he would do if he ran a music school. The more grandiose the theories grew, the more certain he was that he would never have a chance to put them into effect. But some of them were destined to form the basis of a revolution in musical education.

The reputation of Sarah Lawrence's music department and of William Schuman as a teacher spread. In 1938 *Modern Music* published Schuman's article, *Unconventional Case History*, in which he described how a student had proceeded naturally by cultivating her own interests of the moment rather than being forced to follow the accepted chronology of theory instruction. In the course of the article he wrote: "Obviously no one method previously determined can serve everyone with equal effectiveness. With such an approach to education one rules out from the start the kind of indoctrination by which traditional and formal procedures nourish smug acquiescences." Schuman taught with zest, but by 1945, zest was beginning to yield to restlessness and he was open to an offer from G. Schirmer, his publishers.

Schuman's first contact with Schirmer, early in 1932, had been as a fledgling composer seeking a market for his *Chorale Canons*. The Schirmer representative dismissed the fledgling without reading the score on the grounds that there was no market for canons. A second encounter with Schirmer, in 1938, proved more rewarding. Schuman's *Prologue* was accepted, and acceptance led to the composer's first meeting with Carl Engel, president of the firm and its director of publication, who was to play a major role in his career. In commenting on *Prologue* Engel said, "I am not sure I understood it all, but I was intrigued by it. Welcome to the house."

When Engel heard the Carnegie Hall performance of Symphony No. III (1941) he spoke in hyperboles. He believed that there was no one in the world with whom Schuman should study, that the composer had himself become a technical master. He invited Schuman to his home and Schuman steered the conversation to the urgent problem of how, despite the pressures of earning a living, he could find enough hours for composing. Engel promised to ask Schirmer's Board of Directors for permission to pay Schuman a monthly stipend, so that Schuman could teach less and compose more. The permission was granted; there was no contract, just a gentleman's agreement.

In 1942 Schuman submitted to Engel a number of works for chorus: *Requiescat, Holiday Song,* and the *Chorale Canons* that Schirmer had once turned down. Engel accepted them all, singling out the canons as the pieces he particularly liked. He suggested that the title be changed to Four Canonic Choruses. At this meeting, Engel also asked Schuman to give Schirmer the "first refusal" on everything he wrote. "If we turn it down you will be free to take it elsewhere, but you would be foolish if you did", Engel said playfully. Schuman never took anything elsewhere. From that day on, Schirmer accepted everything he submitted.

Schuman could always turn to Engel for emotional support. When Schuman volunteered for the army and was turned down because of a muscular difficulty in his arms, Engel encouraged him to find an outlet in music and gave him the idea that took form as the *Prayer in Time of War* (originally called *Prayer-1943*).[1] Early in 1944 Engel began to talk enigmatically about formalizing

---

[1] Schuman's *Three-Score Set,* which totals sixty measures, was written in honor of Carl Engel's sixtieth birthday.

their agreement. "Perhaps I shall retire to write fairy tales", he said one evening. Another time it was: "If I'm not around, you can always call on Francis Gilbert."[1] A formal agreement between Schuman and Schirmer was executed.

On May 6 of that year Carl Engel died suddenly. When Mrs. J. Philip Benkard, formerly Mrs. Rudolph Schirmer and in 1944 vice-president of G. Schirmer, Inc., consulted Koussevitzky about a successor to Engel as director of publication, the conductor recommended Schuman. Schuman was offered the appointment. He accepted. At his request he was given the time to finish his academic year at Sarah Lawrence, working at Schirmer's meanwhile in his free time.

By now Schuman was the recipient of many musical honors. There were two Guggenheim Fellowships, a grant-in-aid from the Metropolitan Opera Association, the Koussevitzky Foundation Award, the Composition Award offered by the Academy of Arts and Letters. And there had been a trio of firsts. To the joint award by Town Hall and the League of Composers (for the Third String Quartet) and the award by the Music Critics' Circle of New York (for the Third Symphony) was added the first Pulitzer Prize ever to be offered in music (for *A Free Song*).

He could count five symphonies to his credit, a piano concerto, three string quartets, many choral and miscellaneous pieces. There was scarcely a major symphony orchestra, a choral organization, a chamber music group in the country that hadn't at one time or another played something of his. On the West Coast he had found two notable champions, one a conductor, the other a critic. The conductor, Pierre Monteux, had given the *American Festival Overture* and Symphony No. III repeated performances with the San Francisco Symphony Orchestra and was in the future to go so far in admiration as to conduct the Chicago

---

[1] The Schirmer attorney.

Symphony Orchestra in a special Schumann-Schuman concert. The critic, Alfred Frankenstein, had written in *Modern Music* of December 1944 that "The evidence is accumulating on all sides and the conclusion is inevitable: William Schuman has caught the boat";—that "Schuman is closer to Roy Harris, with whom he once studied, than to anyone else, although he has much more rhythmic fire, variety, and vivacity than Harris";—that "the lithe and aerated draughtsmanship of Schuman's polyphony and the luminous quality of his orchestration, which always glows and never glitters—these things, plus the rhythmic variety, gives this music its own strong profile";—that "Enthusiasm is the word for Schuman, and his faults are the faults of enthusiasm. Some of his virtues stem from the same quality, and no one who has written about him has failed to observe it in one way or another." Bernstein noted his "buoyancy", "energetic drive", "vigor of propulsion", and "lust for life"; Paul Rosenfeld, "his force, originally fixed and deadly, which is subjected to a new incarnation and finally moves joyously unified and with a gesture of embrace out towards life".

He had also been heard in foreign parts, including Paris, Vancouver, Antwerp, Oslo, Copenhagen, Brussels, Berlin, Toronto, Mexico City, and the capitals of South America. Among the compositions most frequently played were *American Festival Overture*, *A Free Song*, Symphony for Strings, *Undertow*, and Symphony No. III.

European critics became aware of him. William Glock of The Observer, for one, spent four days at the Library of the American Embassy in London discovering Schuman. On September 2, 1945, at a time when newspapers and space in them were stringently rationed in England, Glock devoted a 15-inch column to Schuman's music. His final sentence was: "Schuman, who writes without any dullness or half-measure should, if not spoiled by success, become a major figure."

If Frankenstein and Glock, and occasionally Downes and Thomson, sang Schuman's praises, other critics felt there was nothing to sing about. B. H. Haggin of *The Nation* was one day to summarize his own attitude towards Schuman and composers like him with the remark that "Excessive tolerance has enabled some of them to get away with murder".

The same violent and contrasted reactions came from the public. Fan letters came from all over the country. The most grandiloquent one came on Schuman's thirty-ninth birthday: "To the great master to wish him long life." But there were other letters, attacking him—some sent to radio stations that broadcast his music and at least one succinct birthday greeting which said, "Why don't you stop writing music?"

On June 1, 1945, Schuman settled down into his Schirmer post with a three-year contract as director of publication. For perhaps the first time in the history of music publishing a major American publisher had chosen a prolific and very active composer as head of its publication department. The event was expected to have significant repercussions on the country's entire musical life. But seven days after Schuman took over the new post, his full-time career in it was threatened.

The perpetrators of the threat were James Warburg and John Erskine, who were members of the Board of Directors of the Juilliard School of Music and who independently had arrived at the name of William Schuman as a candidate for the presidency of the School to succeed the retiring Ernest Hutcheson. Warburg, whose daughter Kay studied with Schuman at Sarah Lawrence, knew him as a teacher at once sound and stimulating. Erskine, serving for a short time as one of the directors of G. Schirmer, came to know Schuman as a composer whose works were making a remarkable impression throughout the country. Moreover, Erskine remembered an encounter with Schuman some months before at a forum on modern music conducted by The New School for Social Research. There Erskine, speaking with his usual force and grace, had concluded with the remark

Schuman, 1943

Schuman and Koussevitzky, 1944

William and Frances Schuman, 1944

Chris Alexander

Martha Graham as Judith, 1951

that modern music presents two problems—that it isn't heard and that it is. To this Schuman had replied provocatively. After expressing his admiration for Erskine's books and his charm as a lecturer, he took up Erskine's remark that music was a language that must communicate directly and criticized his definition of communication as a very limiting one. He went on to disagree with almost everything Erskine had said, but disagreed in the open and urbane manner that characterizes Schuman when he is addressing an audience. Erskine held no grudge. He, in fact, left the meeting with a distinctly favorable impression of Schuman. And that this should be so was a tribute to Erskine's sportsmanship and insight.

For different reasons, then, but with equal fervor, with each eager to place Juilliard in the hands of a new generation, Warburg and Erskine decided to promote Schuman's candidacy. When Warburg asked Schuman whether the idea appealed to him the reply was: "I'm afraid I'm not interested." Actually, though, it was not lack of interest in becoming the head of one of the foremost music schools in the world that had motivated Schuman's reply. Schuman demurred only because he was certain that he would not be given a free hand to do with the presidency what he would want to do with it. Nevertheless Warburg was able to persuade him to meet with the Juilliard Board, which included also Ernest Hutcheson, Edward Johnson, then general manager of the Metropolitan Opera Company, Henry S. Drinker, a lawyer who has translated the vocal works of Bach and other masters, John Perry, who had been Mr. Juilliard's lawyer, and three other eminent attorneys—Parker McCollester, Allen Wardwell, and Franklin B. Benkard.

At the meeting Schuman did not temporize. He said what he thought, good and bad, stating frankly that he thought the School could be improved by a change of policy in this direction and that. Particularly did he suggest a drastic change in the attitude towards composition and theory in the basic structure of the

School's curriculum. After the meeting Johnson congratulated him on not pulling any punches. Drinker also pressed Schuman's hand approvingly.

Official notice of the appointment, to take effect October 1, 1945, came in a letter from the Juilliard Board of Directors. Gustave Schirmer, who had succeeded Carl Engel as president of the publishing firm, released Schuman from his contract as of the following October, but requested that he continue with the firm as chief adviser on publications. Schuman did so, and it was not until more than six years later (January 1, 1952) that the pressure of his other duties led him to resign.

The future president of Juilliard met the press. His forthright personality sizzled and blazed. The man from *Time* summed up the situation: "It is like a *New Republic* editor taking over *The Saturday Evening Post*." The press went home to write its story and the story varied in the telling. In one paper Schuman emerged as a maestro in playclothes, a prexy in loud sports jackets and other Esquirish attire, looking no older than his students. But in another paper he became a prophet of music coming among us at the war's close to indicate conclusively that there had been regenerative influences at work during the dark years.

Schuman's friends were worried. They warned him to compose every day. The warning was needless. In the first five years of his presidency Schuman turned out two dance scores for Martha Graham *(Night Journey,* commissioned for the Harvard Symposium on Music Criticism by the Elizabeth Sprague Coolidge Foundation in the Library of Congress, and *Judith,* commissioned by the Louisville Philharmonic Society); Symphony No. VI, commissioned by the Dallas Symphony League; String Quartet No. IV, commissioned by the Elizabeth Sprague Coolidge Foundation in honor of the 150th anniversary of the Library of Congress; a Violin Concerto commissioned by Samuel Dushkin; *George Washington Bridge,* a band piece written to fulfill a promise to band leaders in the schools and colleges of Michigan; and an *a cappella* chorus, *Truth Shall Deliver: A Ballade of Good Advice*, written for Marshall Bartholomew and the Yale Glee Club.

One of the methods by which Schuman sought to extend the orbit of Juilliard's influence was to arrange exciting programs to be performed by School forces.[1] His internal reforms included the immediate unification of the Juilliard Graduate School and the Institute of Musical Art, numerous personnel changes, and a revamping of the curriculum. Schuman appointed Norman Lloyd as director of education,[2] Mark Schubart, of the music staff of the New York Times, as director of public activities,[3] and combed his memory for others he wanted to bring to Juilliard—Robert Shaw, Thor Johnson, Peter Mennin, William Bergsma, Robert Ward, Vincent Persichetti, Richard Franko Goldman, and others.

Both Lloyd and Schubart were adherents of the cause of enlightened music education and supported Schuman's decision to replace the old theory department with a new department—Literature and Materials of Music. The new department, introduced in Schuman's third year as president, is the core of the curriculum. It has remained constant in its philosophy but has varied from time to time in its organization and procedures. It is an expression of Schuman's search to overcome the inadequacy of routine theory instruction. He has said:

Conventional courses in music theory have failed to educate... The completion of a series of abstract graded exercises has

---

[1] Some highlights of the first few years of Schuman's presidency were the Hindemith festival in honor of that composer's 50th birthday, an Ernest Bloch festival, a festival of contemporary French music, a concert by the School orchestra and chorus in Carnegie Hall with Koussevitzky conducting, an operatic performance of Stravinsky's *Oedipus Rex*, and the first American performance of Britten's version of *The Beggar's Opera*, as well as many performances of major American works. He also established the Juilliard Quartet (Robert Mann and Robert Koff, violins; Raphael Hillyer, viola; Arthur Winograd, 'cello), whose concerts, both at home and abroad, have proved spectacularly successful.

[2] Lloyd has since resigned from this post but continues to teach at the School.

[3] Schubart became dean on July 1, 1949.

come to be substituted for the study of music itself . . . Most of our professional musicians who have been trained in "systems" of harmony are rather ill-informed about the compositional techniques of the music they perform . . . There are in our schools today advanced students of, say, violin, who are relatively unaware of the piano parts in the sonata they are studying . . . In many schools at the present time, as in the past, students are trained in music theory, including diatonic and chromatic harmony, "species" counterpoint, keyboard harmony, dictation, and sight singing, and complete their formal music education with but a slight acquaintance with the literature of music, with little awareness even of the scope of the literature for their own instrument or voice . . . In the exaggerated importance conventional theory education attaches to such a device as dictation we have a clear example of techniques becoming ends in themselves . . . It would seem that conventional theory education shows a consistent lack of concern with the entire work of art, and it is largely because of this that it has failed to develop intelligent listening on the part of musicians . . . If we are to achieve a meaningful transfer of theoretical knowledge into practical performance conventional methods must necessarily fail us.

The new department as core of the curriculum is also in keeping with Schuman's insistence that Juilliard graduates must be not only expert performers, but enlightened musicians and responsible adults.

There was opposition, of course, based partly on the old guard's suspicion of young men in high places and partly on a frank skepticism as to the validity of any music study aside from actual performance. Even Erskine, Schuman's champion, felt during these early days that perhaps Schuman, acting with headlong recklessness, tended to make up his mind too quickly. Erskine's faith in Schuman never wavered, but he wished fervently that Schuman would proceed less precipitously.

The program met with frequent misunderstanding, a misunderstanding that is evidenced by the many requests received at the school for teachers who can "give" the Juilliard Literature and Materials "system", as though this were some educational give-away program or some mail-order product. The very phraseology of these requests is a denial of the spirit of the new program, a spirit concerned with the inner development of students and not with the cheap formalization of a method.

There were students, at first, who were uneasy. This came home to Schuman when, during the early weeks of the Literature and Materials courses, he visited one of the classes. The instructor was giving an analysis of a two-part invention of Bach during which the subject of implied harmonic texture was discussed. The class seemed bewildered because the instructor accepted as equally valid two quite different interpretations given by students. As the instructor went on to show that Bach had not actually given the harmony and that only if he had, could we know with certainty what it was; that both points were valid since the discussion was a theoretical one concerning not what existed but what was implied, Schuman noticed a student squirming uncomfortably. Silent until now, the young man suddenly interrupted the instructor and spoke up bluntly, "Do you mind telling me how this will help me play my horn?"

Schuman, who had been sitting at the back of the room as unobtrusively as possible, slipped out unobtrusively, too. But he left with one clear impression—that the world was desperately in need of expanding mental horizons and the way to begin with musicians was to make sure that in music, at least, their horizons went further than the ends of their horns.

These first insights have proved sound. The brilliant intuition of the energetic novice at Sarah Lawrence and the headlong experimenting of Juilliard's new and enthusiastic president have produced valid concepts for education. Growing mellow, looking back on these experiments while still in the midst of them and while still planning new ones, Schuman is convinced that:

To improve education takes more than dissatisfaction with the status quo . . . the evolution of a curriculum requires willingness to deal not only with the unknown, but with the inconvenient . . . what is required is a profound disrespect for the clerical end of educational accounting (number of hours and points per course, transfer credits, etc; etc.) and a determination to make such inescapable chores bend to an educational ideal and not to permit them to block it.[1]

To the charge that this new program lacks permanent values because its emphasis falls on the changing nature of the art of music, on exploration, on a distaste for "Rules", Schuman makes firm rejoinder:

We are convinced that the values inherent in our approach to music education not only are permanent and absolute, but, in fact, parallel those values idealized by a free society.—It is our responsibility to help the student to see the music of any given period in the light of its own social, political, and cultural climate; to understand that the esthetic laws and technical considerations of one period cannot be imposed upon another; to make known to the student the varying convictions of leading musicians, both past and present, in order to help him to make his own judgments; to learn that art is not concerned with conformity; to equip the student to deal with the novel without ridicule or fear of its strangeness, yet without being impressed by sheer novelty, and with the ability to probe the depths of the unfamiliar. Teaching dedicated to these ideals helps the young musician to form the habit of assuming responsibility for the continuation of his own learning. If the student truly absorbs the concept of free inquiry in the field of music, unimpeded by blind adherence to doctrine and tradition, he will bring something of this approach not only to other fields of knowledge but to the conduct of his daily life. Since a free society can grow only through the process of free inquiry by its citizens, it is my profound hope that the basic attitudes instilled through the Literature and Materials program will lead to the maturity of the musician and help towards his enlightenment as a citizen in a democracy.[1]

What Schuman has done at Juilliard has aroused widespread interest and not a few of the observers who have come from schools and colleges throughout the country to see the program in action have gone home to report favorably about it. Recognition of a high order came in June 1949 when Schuman received an honorary degree,

---

[1] *The Juilliard Report on Teaching the Literature and Materials of Music,* New York: W. W. Norton & Co., 1953.

that of Doctor of Music, from the University of Wisconsin —the youngest person so honored in the century since the University was founded. Conferring the degree, the president of the University summed up in these words the young man who had returned from Salzburg a musical unknown fourteen years before: "We recognize in you a composer of originality, imagination, and resourcefulness; a director of a celebrated music school with challenging ideas in musical education; a distinguished leader of contemporary American composition, who has already given many and varied important compositions to the world of music."

III

IN THE HOUSEHOLD of William and Frances Schuman in New Rochelle any morning can be felt the excitement with which Schuman gets ready for a new day. Each day for him must somehow be a "great" day exuberantly lived—each day must be all its hours.

This heightened sense of living, of getting things done, made possible his achievements despite his late start as a composer. His Faustian restlessness has always propelled him on. Time is a commodity to be hoarded, an enemy to be conquered, a friend to be cultivated. Schuman himself is a personality seldom in repose. Roy Harris put it this way: "I can't imagine Bill's spending one minute contemplating a rose."

The late start had another important influence. It meant that the bedrock of Schuman's personality was firmly set before he ever thought of himself as an artist. He could not uproot the twenty-odd years that had preceded his decision to become a composer, nor suddenly cultivate an estheticism altogether extraneous to his already molded personality. For this reason he is free of two of the most baffling problems confronting artists—a sense of isolation from average people, and an ineptitude in the conduct of practical affairs. Once a "real boy", later a "regular guy", smooth, effective as an organizer, he is, and always has been, the very reverse of the popular picture of the artist as long-haired, gauche, living a life of penury, beating ineffectual wings. Though musically he became a radical, he clung to conservative manners.

Schuman is relatively free of introspection and of psychic conflict. He was able to change the whole course of his life without wasting much energy in self-reproach or foreboding. But nonetheless the restlessness that spurred his ambition remains to deprive him of simple quietude. He cannot empty his mind of ideas and responsibilities and let a wise passivity fill it.

Schuman is a pragmatist. His pragmatism is a way of asserting his ego effectively in the world of practical affairs and it is also a form of altruism, the altruism of promoting causes. It is a pragmatism strongly colored by moral and ethical convictions. The ethical emphasis instilled by his family has never left him and has made it difficult for him to make compromises. The artist, he feels, must function with equal effectiveness in his world of music, paints, or words and in the everyday world. The artist must never use his art as license for eccentricity, erotic privilege, or violation of ethical principles. One need not be a good man to be a good artist but just because a man is a good artist he cannot be excused for his shortcomings as a human being. The man and his art must be judged independently, the case resting on the separate evidence each presents. Schuman knew that he himself could not become an effective artist unless he freed himself from economic worry. His solution was to become his own patron through teaching so that his music could be free of commercial necessity and therefore of commercial dictates. If an artist is to be his own patron, he must earn a living; and if he is to earn a living, he must cultivate skills and behavior patterns that are acceptable. To live within the given, one must make peace with the Philistines, and to make peace one must make all unimportant concessions. One can do this and yet remain uncompromising on the real issues.

At the same time, he believes that the best strategy is to be frank. In the early 'forties, he used to give lectures on music. Once in Pittsburgh he blasted the music critics. When he noticed a critic in the front row, he paused a moment and then shot at his mark: "You may think because you are here, nodding your head, that I don't mean you. But I do!" This frankness he also shows in his relations with his associates. He wants them to know where they stand in relation to him. Yet, as an administrator or teacher he believes in showing respect for other people's egos rather than in parading his own.

Pragmatism necessitates adjustment and Schuman functions the way an adjusted man should. His adjustment is, in fact, a form of dynamic optimism which synchronizes with the American character and the American dream. In the 1920s, when America was on an extended binge, Schuman was growing up and his natural, boyish prankishness coincided with the spirit of the era. In the 'thirties, the American mood had changed; sobriety was the order of the day; and now, too, Schuman's personality had naturally passed through a metamorphosis and was in harmony with the new seriousness. This parallel between his evolving personality and the spirit of the period in which he was coming of age is in part merely an accident of chronology. But only in part. It expresses a delicate attunement with his time and his place. A later symbol of this attunement can be found in the fact that when Schuman lived in New York City during the first years of his marriage, he found impetus in the pressure of four walls and the pulse of the city. But no sooner had he moved to the country—first to Larchmont, then to New Rochelle—than he saw that the impetus could just as readily come from quiet, detachment, and tree-dotted landscapes.

The adjustment is also that of a man who is a good animal and has lived a normal and happy family life. Mrs. Schuman has always made his career the center of their lives, yet has managed to maintain a measure of independence. She held her job as counsellor at the Vocational Advisory Service until three weeks before their son, Anthony William, was born (December 22,

1943). Schuman, who has never had any use for parasites, economic, emotional, or intellectual, has respected this independence. His nature has demanded both objectivity and emotional support and his wife has given him both. He has an almost stern sense of duty in family matters. When Tony was born, the first thing Schuman said to his wife in the hospital was: "Now I'll have to make a will."

Schuman enjoys the father role, dramatizes it, and even sometimes indulges in it with people other than Tony or Andrea, his adopted daughter who became part of the Schuman household when Tony was five-and-a-half and she, five months. Schuman talks animatedly of putting Tony and Andrea to bed with stories about the instruments of the orchestra illustrated by every kind of music, including of course a liberal sampling of jazz, and of how Tony at five-and-a-half showed musical astuteness. Once while Schuman was working on *Night Journey,* Tony wandered into the study. Schuman sang him a measure but Tony shook his head, saying "Make it more scary, daddy". Schuman did as directed and claims the change was for the better. Andrea at four improvised dances to her father's improvisations at the piano.

There are some artists who, more normally abnormal, resent Schuman strongly. To them he seems *too* well-adjusted to be an artist at all. His integration strikes them as sterility, his ability to get along with people of different types, as Philistinism. These artists resent him for being acceptable and successful. He will admit that his is a success story but not in the strict sense, insisting that it is rather the story of artistic success urgently sought but of increased earnings coming unpredictably. "I'm glad I was never poor", he says, "so I've never had any respect for wealth." On the whole he takes a matter-of-fact view of his achievement, attributing this achievement to hard work, to the right teachers, and above all to a positive refusal to take "No" for an answer. He explains his career as a musical administrator in equally realistic terms: there is a great difficulty in filling administrative posts in music; many musicians are temperamentally unsuited to this kind of work; he, as it happens, is well suited to it. He is also well suited to seeing music in relation to the other arts and in relation to its world role. Recognition of this ability came when, in September 1952, the State Department chose him to represent American music at an International Conference of Creative Artists sponsored by UNESCO and held in Venice. Literature, theater and movies, architecture, painting, and sculpture were the other fields represented; Thornton Wilder was chairman of the American delegation and Schuman vice-chairman.

He is sometimes surprisingly humble, as when, talking of outstanding men of affairs such as the Juilliard Board of Directors, he will say: "It is not given in the normal life of a musician to meet men of that caliber. Being president of Juilliard has meant the opportunity of knowing these men and men like them and I'm grateful." He is likely to become awed in the presence of an authority on a subject of which he has only a layman's knowledge.

Yet there are many subjects in which he qualifies as the intelligent layman. A regular reader of such publications as *Harper's, The New Republic,* and of England's *New Statesman and Nation,* a faithful reader of the Times and the Herald Tribune, reading real estate page, financial figures, baseball scores, everything, he is conversant with contemporary events and opinion. These events he watches from a position in the middle of the road. To establish the exact position on that road one might describe his political and social philosophy as Rooseveltian. He has remained a consistent, if at times highly critical, admirer of the late president. Yet, at each election he gives the matter of voting for a Republican real consideration—as should be the habit of one who was named after William Howard Taft.

Interested in the improvement of man's lot, he believes in every safeguard to preserve the identity of the individual while the improvement is being effected. It is shortsighted, he holds, to attempt to improve man's lot and to forfeit freedom in the attempt by yielding to social control from either the left or the right. Despite the wretched condition of the world, the world has made progress, he believes, a progress clearly measurable in education, housing, in food and in health. Suspicious of Utopias with their panaceas, he thinks that man can improve his lot only in slow time.

He reads a wide variety of books, biography, poetry—especially new poetry—, economics, history, medicine, semantics, psychology, as the subject happens to catch his fancy. He has time for novels only in the summer. When he reads fiction he gets so involved in the story that he can't put the book down. The only books that really bore him are routine musicological studies. He is fascinated by such works as Berlioz's *Mémoires*.

He goes to some sixty or seventy concerts a year—many of them Juilliard concerts. He was once a record collector but stopped when he started teaching. Now he studies scores instead of buying records. He doesn't go to the opera often, but he has his favorites: *Carmen,* any opera by Mozart, Verdi's *Otello.* Nothing could induce him to sit through *Parsifal,* although once he had his Wagner period.

He is in love with the theater. He loves it when it is high art and he loves it when it is out and out commercial. His most excited theater memories are of plays by Ibsen and Chekhov, *The Green Bay Tree,* and the productions of the Group Theatre, especially plays by Clifford Odets. In the theater and in literature he finds great emotional excitement, the same sort of excitement that he finds in music itself.

Movies are something else. He likes to cry with the tortured and exult with the victorious. He expects nothing and always gets a lot, perhaps as much out of a bad picture as out of a good one if the picture is really bad enough.

He insists on catholicity of taste as a practical necessity and believes that works of all schools must be put on trial before the bar of public opinion. In spite of the fact that the esthetic ideals of Roger Sessions's music are quite different from his own, he recommended the publication of Sessions's Symphony No. 2 by Schirmer and was indirectly responsible for the recording of that symphony through a Naumburg Foundation subsidy.

Schuman is given to sharp changes of personality. He is often animated by an extreme impetuousness that leads him to gamble on many a crucial matter. But the gamble is undertaken only after intense and exhaustive examination of the odds. Sometimes the impetuousness leads him into a high enthusiasm which swiftly develops into a lost enthusiasm, leaving those whom he involved in it dazed and forgotten on the sidelines. He is sentimental. When he is away from home, he gets homesick as easily as a child. Florida Chatman, the Schumans' maid, thinks of him primarily as a kind man who has taken time to teach her to play the piano and to open other avenues of knowledge to her. At a concert Schuman has excused himself from a bevy of bigwigs to seek out Max Persin, his old harmony teacher. "He was always a kind boy, with a sense of gratitude", Persin has remarked. Discovering talent in a student whose composition he heard at the High School of Music and Art, Schuman sought out the boy and taught him gratis for years. When Schuman left Sarah Lawrence, it was important that Mrs. Schuman take his picture with his beloved colleague Miss Warren. He still regrets the loss of the intimate touch he had with students in the Sarah Lawrence days.

His close friends in the music world have a way of becoming his professional associates and professional associates have a way of becoming his close friends.

For an avowed realist he is curiously intuitive and impressionable. It was intuition that inspired most of his appointments. One night, in a Scarsdale movie theater, he happened to see Benjamin Grasso and remembered having met him once before at a meeting of music educators. On the strength of a favorable recollection of the man, Schuman felt certain that he would make the perfect educational director for Schirmer. The hunch was confirmed by subsequent conversations, and on Schuman's recommendation Grasso got the job. No less spontaneous was Schuman's recommendation that Nathan Broder, manager of Schirmer's advertising department, be promoted to manager of the publication department. Or that a new and important post, that of director of symphonic and dramatic repertory, be created at Schirmer's for Hans Heinsheimer, who was leaving Boosey and Hawkes. He had not seen Heinsheimer for ten years but a favorable impression lingered. Significantly, Schuman's hunches, whether at Juilliard or Schirmer's, have proved sound. His appointees have in the main been brilliant successes. He seeks able men, gives them authority to work independently, and evaluates them in terms of intensive criticism, positive and negative. And, in return, he seeks the same kind of evaluation from them.

These men are like him in their dedication to the cause of new music. He is always on the offensive, finding jobs for people, and is fond of telling those he believes in that they should be an influence wherever they can help the cause. They will seek his advice and he is fond of giving it. There are those musicians who stand by in boyish hero worship, saying: "I can do more because Bill Schuman believes in me." There are others who say: "He's important to me. I don't know whether I'm important to him." Some are envious of him. Some are imitative. Once at a party when there was talk of a certain young composer's work someone remarked that it was "all William Schuman". Schuman replied jokingly: "It is nice to know that some people have the good sense to move in that general direction."

He loves gadgets like meatslicers and ice-cream makers and is quite likely to insist on having a strawberry ice-cream soda on a freezing February night. He enjoys experimenting with startling combinations in food. Just to tease a Babbitt he will say: "Artistic people ought to be allowed to eat more than other people."

Yet there is also a severity about him, a refusal to tolerate people who play at music, or, for that matter, at any other art. Unrelenting is his contempt for a certain brand of intellectualism which he considers pretentious and arty. In his definition music becomes pretentious when it crosses the line between a direct expression of human emotion and a devious expression of an affected attitude towards life. The word "arty" from his lips has the same ring of disparagement as "atheist" would have from the mouth of a bishop.

Driving himself hard, he has driven others hard, too, insisting that everyone and everything around him be faultless, perhaps faultily faultless. He is impatient with people who do not rise to the occasion and is exacting with people who work under him. His anger will be aroused by a typographical error in a Juilliard program note, or by a Philharmonic program note saying: "William Schuman who lives in Larchmont." But in the last case, at least, the annoyance may be suddenly dispelled in a burst of humor: "When they don't keep their notes up to date, it makes you feel like a standard composer." Humor, the conversational light touch, the unexpected turn of a sentence, are characteristic.

When people warn Schuman that his life as an administrator and his life as a composer are in disharmony, he refuses to accept their premise. Who is there better than a composer to insure that performing musicians are taught that musical execution must always be in terms of the technical and esthetic dictates of the composition performed? Is not the composer's training the core training in music? If Berlioz and Robert Schumann could be critics as well as composers, what is wrong with a composer's being an administrator and educator, especially when he happens to enjoy even the mundane details of running a large school? Or, for that matter,

Schuman with Barber, Copland, Thomson, and Menotti, 1952

John Stewart

A page from the autograph manuscript of Schuman's Violin Concerto

with a composer's helping to shape the policies of music publishing? Isn't the composer-administrator-educator combination just as natural as the composer-critic combination?

A small college recently offered to pay him well to handle a job that would leave him many free hours in which to compose. He turned it down, knowing that he would instinctively try to turn the small job into a big one because the administrator is a part of his personality, just as the composer is part. The two are simply different phases and both must be in operation if he is to be happy. Education he sees as a great drama and romance and would not want to be removed from it. And while he is envious of composers who have endless free time for their work, there is no solution for his envy. For he would not be happy with endless free hours in which to compose and do nothing else.

In originating ideas and projects for Juilliard or Schirmer, the Naumburg Foundation, the Koussevitzky Music Foundation, the Advisory Committee on American Music for Columbia Records, or the several other organizations with which he has been connected, he feels the same kind of awakening that he finds in composing itself. This same quickening comes, too, during his many talks to students and faculty, appearances as an after-dinner speaker, or, more formally, as a speaker before music teachers' associations, forums on educational problems, and commemorative occasions. To speaking he brings his usual theatrical flair, timing his laughs like an actor and like an actor giving the illusion of effortlessness. This, along with his ready talent for improvisation and his flexibility in adjusting his manner to suit many different kinds of audiences, makes his talks seem to many of his colleagues like crisp, clean air blowing through musty academic corridors.

Yet these other passionate interests do not, he firmly believes, detract from the quality of his work as a composer. His composing has not suffered because he is an administrator, nor has he been less the administrator because he is a composer. Quality, he will tell you, has to do with standards and standards are not destroyed by extending the range of your activities. He admits that there has been a quantitative loss—as a composer in the number of compositions he turns out; as an administrator in the number of outside obligations he is able to assume. Should he allow himself to get political and become involved in doing all the things a career administrator must do, he knows his music would suffer, for there just wouldn't be time for it. But the music becomes the brake, holding him back, keeping him within the musical fold.

He will listen to criticism and says that it is silly not to do so because through criticism he may learn something. He believes that talk of the content of instrumental music in terms of a direct, calculated extra-musical expression is nonsense. He is unhappy when not writing music and he writes it for the same reason that he once played baseball—because he finds it exciting.

When he writes, he shuts out everything else. If he is called to the 'phone, he will come right back and pick up where he left off. Later, the return to the workaday world is quite easy. He works regularly—if pressed, on a strict schedule, after meticulously planning a chart of hours and faithfully punching a self-imposed time clock. People always ask him: "How can you be sure you'll accomplish anything when you work without inspiration?" He answers: "Of course you don't know whether you'll turn it out if you do work. But you can be sure you won't turn it out if you don't work."

He refuses to put anything on paper until it actually moves him. Many composers indicate precise tempos and dynamics in their score only after a work is completed. He starts with tempo first, adjusting his metronome at a certain speed and thinking as it goes. He does comparatively little rewriting; in Symphony No. VI, for instance, only the final page and some editorial changes.

Occasionally, however, he may become dissatisfied with an entire movement and withdraw the work for revision.

He writes for the instruments of the orchestra directly, not through a preliminary piano sketch. He sings the parts at the top of his lungs, preferring this method to playing the parts on the piano because his music is essentially melodic and because he sings better than he plays. He doesn't play any instrument very well. He does, however, use the piano for new vocabulary departures; that is, for experimentation.

How does a work get started? The incentive for Symphony No. VI, for instance, was a commission from the Dallas Symphony League. In May 1948, Schuman knew he had to have a new work for a Dallas première in February 1949. He planned a Divertimento, several short pieces in the manner of a "pops" concert, and later changed the prospective title to *Fair Park* to honor the auditorium where it would be produced. Until June the idea dwelt in the warm dark. During June and July he went to his study regularly each morning, attempting to get started. Nothing came. August brought a change. Suddenly, springing full bloom, came a theme that he felt was exquisite. But it bore no relation to the work he had planned. What had come was an idea for a big work. The theme seemed to lead to a symphony and to demand a novel kind of one-movement structure. He was like a playwright with a character who has taken over and is dictating the plot. At this point, he knew he had to abandon the preconceived notion and start once again with the "exquisite" theme as his germ idea.

September was upon him. The opening weeks of the new semester at Juilliard took all his time. The February deadline hung over his head. A rigorous routine was the answer. In order to earn a free Sunday he had to find fifteen free hours during the week: two hours in the morning from eight to ten, or from nine to eleven, at home before going to Juilliard; on Saturdays and holidays all day. The result was Symphony No. VI. A slow beginning, however, did not characterize the inception of **String Quartet No. IV**, which was begun on June 25, 1950, and finished August 3.

And so each day is all its hours and life seems good to him, so good that he is watching his calories because they say thin people live longer and he wants to live long, just as long as possible, because there are so many works he wants to write and there are so many projects he has in mind. More than forty years are behind him—but there are years and years ahead—hours and hours to fill with work. This is the present, this time that is his. And as for the future—well, the future lives in the motion of the present.

End of Part One

which is dedicated by its author

to the memory of

Eugene Gladstone O'Neill, Jr.

Part Two

THE MUSIC

THE STYLE
Creative Bearings

If there is more of one ingredient than another in the rich mixture of William Schuman's music it is the strong-flavored energy that generates a constant boil of movement. There is motion stirred by boldness and intensity, movement that pushes forward resourcefully and seriously, and beneath even the quietest pages a restless current that will eventually surface in a rush.

This youthful drive might well send the music catapulting over any real compositional problems. Sheer speed and quick changes of harmonic garb could carry it along, sidestepping direct solutions. In this most characteristic element of Schuman's music his kindest critics see a potential weakness. Objectivity is often lost in music conceived in such passion, and many an earnest listener is swept on more by fury than by sound. A close study of Schuman's music and a real understanding of his creative approach will, I believe, reveal a solid composer with an original creative spirit.

Much of Schuman's music is linear and its melodic contour forms huge arcs of sound. Lines without the usual phrase-breaths move steadily through an entire section towards a goal well fixed in the composer's mind at the outset. The harmonies that result from this contrapuntal movement do not form a progression from chord to chord or bass note to bass note, but rather weave a pattern of similar chordal structures with matching textures suited to the mood and personality of the musical statement. And by the same token, when the problem is approached harmonically Schuman selects a unifying kind of harmony rather than a bass-regulated series of chords.

The result is a forward-moving mass of sound in unorthodox treatment that is as unfamiliar to some ears as it is peculiar to the Schuman idiom. This music, without structural gaps and recurring cadences, can easily be mistaken for the misguided wanderings of a fundamentally conventional mode of writing. The surest path to the core of Schuman's music and to an understanding of his well-thought-out approach may be through a study of its melodic constituents and singing shape.

Enthusiasm, drive, and bite in a melodic frame give Schuman's music its power of projection. This huge-sounding music is made for billboards rather than newspapers. Boldness, freshness, and intensity of feeling are prominent; yet there is some grace and charm. Most of Schuman's music is about something big. Intimacy and delicacy appear as reflected images of the primary idea, and slip by easily. Only short periods of time are allowed for personal retrospection, and as contrast, the contemplative is overshadowed, or even swallowed, by surrounding passages. Long slow pages seem held in a firm masculine hand, yet sometimes bear the touch of gentleness, as in the Fourth String Quartet, whose first movement remains calm as the lines are led on unruffled by the serene second theme. When the even quieter opening theme is employed as a developing force this work virtually tiptoes. Except for three short agitated places, the closing section is soft and delicate to the end.

In early works Schuman lacked an objective approach. He was terribly anxious to write and loved his measures so fiercely that he was unable to evaluate them fairly. Inferior stuff was mixed with exciting, original material and carried by continuous drive to make the passage come off. Delighted with his ability to produce a variety of colors by combining fourths, he set out to build whole sections and sometimes pieces on these chords by fourths. The harmonic background became pale and the tension monotonous, so that there was a drain on his rhythmic and formal resources which sapped the quality of the output.

Schuman was quick to realize what was happening and

began to demand that his abused harmonic formations take their place in the formal scheme. His structural thinking was imaginative and colorful, and required his harmonies to follow through in reciprocal relation. His palette widened and progress in developing creative perspective was rapid. He was twenty-three years old when he completed his first published serious work, the Four Canonic Choruses. One needs only to look at the Third String Quartet, written barely six years later, to find a maturer Schuman. The Quartet ranks with the best of his output and begins a long line of remarkable compositions.

He does not seek aid from out-of-the-way experiments, those obvious attempts to lure the public to a work by way of an unheard-of combination of instruments or an extramusical association. The press is never able to hail or propagandize a coming Schuman event; they can only announce it. There is no parasiting on a prominent political event, nor are there self-eulogizing program-notes at hand. One attends the performance and finds the excitement in the music.

The Melodic Clue

Schuman's music springs from a single lexicon of thought. Its profile is strong and definite, and there is an over-all clarity. A conductor once dismissed his music with "But I want music with melodies". Schuman replied, "It is all melody. If you can't sing my music it is because you can't sing." This is our clue to understanding his music. Each idea pivots on the melodic. The rhythmic structure is implied in the thematic outlines and the harmonies are suggested by the characteristic melodic skips and general textural feeling. Even form ideas are generated by the physical needs and implications of the primary melody. Ornamental tones in a slow theme will sooner or later be released in a fast section suggested by the embellishments. Or a melody may contain an interval that leaps upward. In development this characteristic skip will be expanded to help it in its reach, and a martial background of polychords might be punched out in assistance. A searching, lyric melody may establish a form in pursuing its winding course to the final cadence. Then again, a tune may have a stubborn tone as its low point, and an entire section may be built around this single tone. A nosediving melody might suggest a background pattern of falling tones to support a new section which will be slow and singing. Melodic implication seems always at the source, and structural derivatives of melodic character form Schuman's music.

He does a great deal of singing while composing. Speaking on a broadcast of his wordless Choral Etude, Schuman hinted at the vocal approach. "Sounds can be sung on syllables uniquely suited to the nature of the music expressed. I feel we all do this subconsciously when we sing a tune without words and supply nonsense syllables. I simply listened to the way in which I sang my own choral music and recorded those sounds phonetically."

He works hard at his craft and knows his materials. Though a young man, he has, in a surprisingly short space of time, developed a personal style. His rhythmic and harmonic gestures are easily distinguished from those of his contemporaries, and his melodies contain unmistakable Schumanesque trade-marks. Even when he appropriated tunes from the 18th century, in the *William Billings Overture,* he took them so thoroughly through his own creative channels that they emerged good Schuman. As to why Schuman sounds like Schuman, perhaps the answer can be found in those personal elements that occur frequently in highly individualized treatment—those qualities that make his music distinctively his own.

In a restless or daring melodic passage consecutively climbing fourths are used for varying degrees of tension:

Ex. 1. Second String Quartet (Fugue)

Consecutive falling fourths and climbing fifths are used for varying degrees of tension in a quiet or contemplative melodic passage. The *ostinato* opening of the Fourth Symphony is essentially quiet, yet searching in spirit:

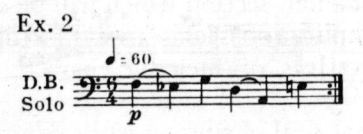

Ex. 2

Fluctuating major and minor thirds are characteristic in calm and tender spots:

Ex. 3. Third String Quartet

However, the minor third descending and returning to the original note as "Wee-Awk-Eee" in the *American Festival Overture* (see Ex. 54) has become a symbol of triumph for Schuman. Larger works tend to culminate with the boyish "Wee-Awk-Eee" transformed into cries of strength. This can be seen in a glance through the last three pages of the Third Symphony.

Initial melodic formations are predominantly diatonic. Chromatic passing tones are noticeably absent:

Ex. 4. Quartettino for Four Bassoons (Fughetta)

The melodic strong points, whether high or low, seldom coincide with the metrical strong beat:

Ex. 5. *Night Journey*

Schuman's melody can grow to astounding length without transcending the listener's powers of melodic perception. Slow melodies tend to be long:

Ex. 6. Symphony for Strings

and often form the basis of a whole work. The fifty-two measure introduction to the Third String Quartet is actually a single melody. Rapid melodies are usually short:

Ex. 7. Quartettino for Four Bassoons (*ostinato*)

but occasionally are long:

Ex. 8. Symphony for Strings (3rd Mvt.)

His melodies can be predominantly angular:

Ex. 9. Violin Concerto

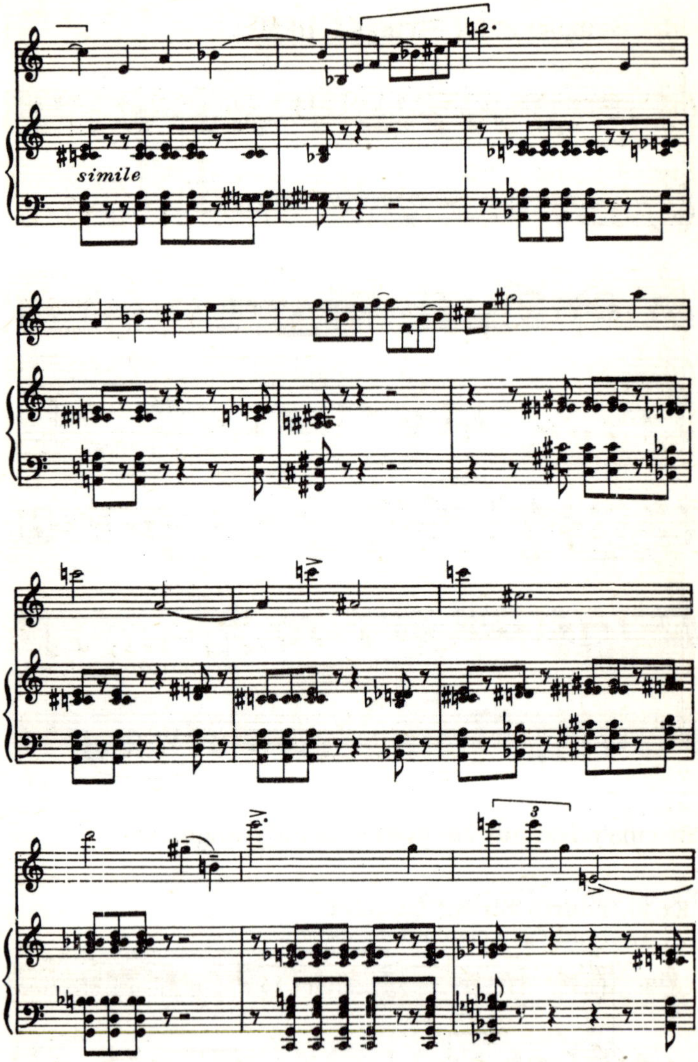
simile
3

or curvy and adventurous:

Ex. 10. Fourth String Quartet

In earlier works, single-line tunes were often supported by strummed, plucked, or held chords; but in the Fourth String Quartet, three and four song-like lines form intriguing folds in the harmonic structure. The leap of the octave is a typical trait and is often used at the opening of a melodic line. Most of the sections from the Secular Cantata No. 1, *This Is Our Time,* begin with the ascending octave:

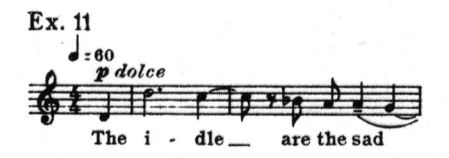

Ex. 11

The i - dle__ are the sad

Harmonic Materials

Schuman does not use tonality for structural purposes. Nevertheless, it is strongly felt in his music, even though there is no key signature. He does not restrict his thinking to major and minor dictates or to a set number of accidentals at the start of a piece. He covers the wide gamut of scales bestowed upon Occidental civilization, and needs the elbow room afforded by the freedom of shifting modes, "twelve-tone" melodies if he chooses, but always a tonality. Even though the first movement of the Fourth String Quartet is not glued fast to a prescribed key, tonality is felt. The "key" is a product of the opening viola tones E-flat and D. These tones introduce the A theme at the beginning, and close the movement by sounding the top tones of the chords in the final cadence. Some of his harmony is misunderstood. The much mentioned polytonality in Schuman is not polytonality but polyharmony. Triads of kindred tonalities joining to form one resonant five- or six-note chord result in a harmony enriched by overtones and belonging to one key. He is fond of these chords and can manipulate them by adjusting the dissonant relationship of the chord-members to acquire any texture he needs.

In the Piano Concerto there are polychordal passages consisting of two species of harmony—a major triad a major sixth above a major triad, and a major triad a minor seventh above a minor triad:

Ex. 12

Polychords are favorites with Schuman. The first four measures of the *Three-Score Set* (second piece) employ triads of different origins simultaneously. They complement each other in such a way that the resulting harmonies are intensely dissonant, yet resonant. The Symphony for Strings (second movement) opens with the same phrase:

Ex. 13

In later works the bottom triad of a polychord is often stripped, leaving only one tone. The new harmony is supple and can be used as a pivot chord so that the composer can move easily from one kind of harmony to another. It is usually a major chord on top with the minor third below, as found in the opening of *Judith* and the Sixth Symphony. But in the fast movements of the Violin Concerto both major and minor thirds appear simultaneously, a minor second apart, and in the slow movement are employed horizontally. This "mijor" or "manor" harmony occasionally moves to consonant harmony but then proves dissonant to the melody.

A definite kind of harmonic texture is used throughout a passage. Several phrases in *A Free Song* consist of alternating major and minor triads:

Ex. 14

In the opening of the *Three-Score Set* for piano, inversions of chords by fourths are used exclusively:

Ex. 15

and in the finale of the Violin Concerto, minor triads:

Ex. 16

Schuman at a UNESCO meeting. Third from left, Malipiero; to Schuman's left, Honegger, Ibert, and Egge

Schuman with his wife and children, Anthony and Andrea

Gloria Hoffman

The street-corner hymn from *Undertow* is first harmonized with major triads exclusively:

Ex. 17

then it is given a polytonal setting (in the drunk scene). Suspensions and appoggiaturas in the second-cornet line cause intervals of the second to form at each change of the melody:

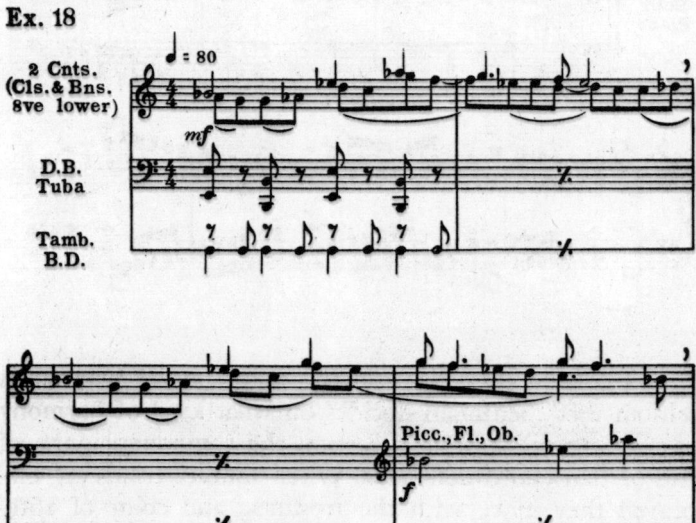

Ex. 18

When the brass is given a religious statement of the "hymn", soft-textured chords are gently ornamented:

Ex. 19

One kind of harmony is used not only for a phrase; it may underlie an entire passage. The following excerpt from the Piano Concerto illustrates a clever handling of ornamental tones and rhythmic flares in order to keep a solitary major seventh chord interesting and pushing forward:

Ex. 20

Harmony with voices moving in the usual manner is seldom used. Schuman decides on what kind of harmony to use, instead of what direction the component parts of this or that chord shall take. When simpler triads are employed they move with the freshness and color of 16th-century music and with the extra benefit of the early 20th-century contributions:

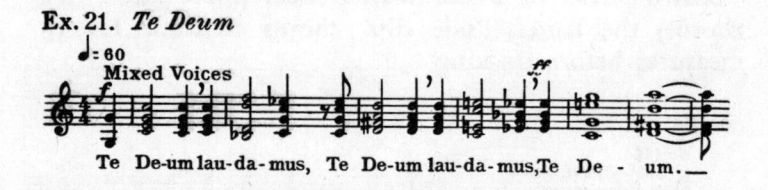

Ex. 21. *Te Deum*

[musical example: Mixed Voices, ♩=60, "Te De-um lau-da-mus, Te De-um lau-da-mus, Te De-um."]

When necessary, his part-writing can be as smooth as any known. The three-part harmony in the woodwind passage of the first movement of the Piano Concerto is a mixture of triads and chords by fourths that produces colorful harmonic movement of this type:

Ex. 22

[musical example: Ob., Fl., Cl., ♩=120, *mf dolce*]

His parallel harmony seldom gets bulky by dragging blocks of chords too far. The parallel chords in *A Free Song* (played by trumpets and trombones) spread out at the end of the phrase:

Ex. 23

[musical example: ♩=132, *ff*]

Occasionally he overdoes parallel motion. He is aware of the danger involved but believes the musical effect well worth the risk. In *Truth Shall Deliver* (three-part men's chorus) the frozen "side slip" chords continue for 19 measures before thawing:

Ex. 24

At - tempt not all things crook-ed to re-dress

But trust in for - tune, turn-ing as a ball;

His sense of harmonic rhythm is strong. One cannot mistake the intended mood. When he is after restlessness the harmony changes often:

Ex. 25. Fourth String Quartet (2nd Mvt.)

Allegro con fuoco

when he wants breadth, the changes are widely spaced:

Ex. 26. Fourth Symphony (2nd Mvt.)

Most pieces end with a triad preceded by almost any possible combination of tones, yet with a feeling of finality as firm as that given by a dominant-tonic cadence:

Ex. 27. Third Symphony (Fugue)

Seldom do pieces end with a dissonant chord. One exception is the first movement of the Second String Quartet, which ends with a thirteenth chord:

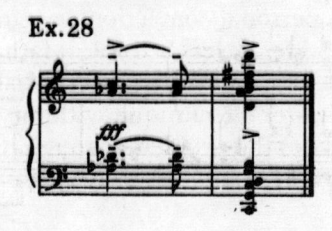

Ex. 28

A piece that has been complex in tonal movement frequently ends in unison. With some composers this sounds like a trick; with Schuman it is a strong resolution:

Ex. 29. Symphony for Strings (1st Mvt.)

Do not search for chords of the dominant seventh, dominant ninth, diminished seventh, or cadential six-four. At these Schuman pales.

"Modernism" is usually associated with harmony. Many contemporary works that are generously supplied with dissonant chords are otherwise quite conventional and are not as new as they sound at first hearing. In Schuman, however, we have not only dissonance, but innovations in the rhythm, form, and melody. His modernism is distinctively individual and unique. In his song-plugging days he heard few of the serious works that were either grafted to jazz idioms or forced into a dissonant shell by experimentalists. He built his own path of dissonant thinking and his ideas were already crystallized by the time he was fully exposed to new trends. He invariably found merit in techniques far removed from his own creative channels, but his personal conviction was such that atonality was rejected. He never became infatuated with the twelve-tone style. His music, however, has the melodic resources of twelve-tone technique without the atonal element. He approaches the problem through juxtaposition of modes, which often results in two sets of harmonies at once.

Rhythmic and Linear Approach

Schuman's music is regarded by his more nationalistic admirers as strongly American in flavor. This is due largely to his rhythmic sense. As Roy Harris once pointed out, Europeans think of rhythm in its largest common denominator, while we are brought up with a feeling for its smallest units. Jazz players are chained to symmetrical dance rhythms but continually break into cross-rhythm variations. This superimposing of rhythm has entered the American blood stream.

Schuman has a way of writing these rhythms without meter changes. The fundamental pulse-beats remain regular for long stretches while the metric patterns above this beat shift constantly. Off beats are often accented, a derivation of jazz. He is fond of this kind of figure, as found in the final movement of the Third String Quartet (the same theme is used for the finale of the Fourth Symphony):[1]

Ex. 30

When metric patterns above the fundamental beat begin shifting, everything bounces. These syncopated passages are part of a cumulative rhythmic scheme. They are never carried far, but come and go freely. This usage is peculiar to Schuman. Ordinarily rhythms of this type start as a quick-step that continues to jiggle to the end of a long section. The following fragment from *Night Journey* is the middle portion of a twenty-two measure passage leading to a fermata:

---

[1] Similar figures may be found in the middle of *Circus Overture* and the first and last movements of the Violin Concerto.

Ex. 31

♩ = 96
Strings & Piano

One does not sense a struggle to find new rhythms in Schuman's music. His jazz career charged him with natural and exciting rhythmic ideas. The only effort expended in this direction is in getting the complicated notation on paper. Unlike the music of some Americans whose sources of style can be traced to jazz, Schuman's reveals jazz elements as an integral part of his thinking; they never obtrude as foreign bodies.[1] These varied rhythms are integrated in large patterns that make up sections. One section grows into the next, resulting in wide sweeps of strident rhythmic masses. The structure of his largest work can stand firmly on its rhythmic elements alone. A characteristic Harris motif is sometimes overused in shoving tired fast passages:

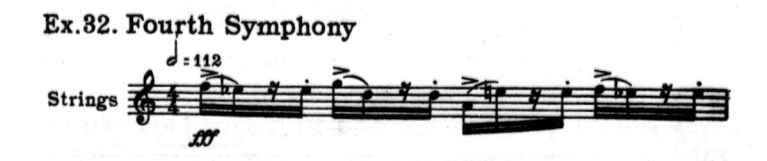

Ex. 32. Fourth Symphony

♩ = 112
Strings

Ostinato rhythms of extreme simplicity can be exciting. The opening theme of the Piano Concerto (finale) is stated by the solo piano over a left-hand ground figure:

---

[1] When Schuman was asked by a student at a lecture in the University of Louisville whether *Judith* did not contain the "influence of jazz", he replied: "That's no influence—that's jazz."

His extensive use of cross rhythms produces a contrapuntal rhythmic structure. The interplay of stresses in this contrapuntal passage from the Third Symphony is fascinating:

Ex. 34

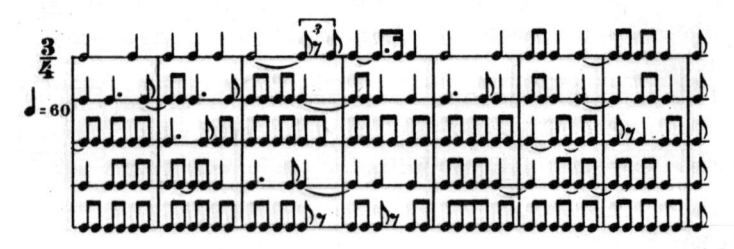

Much of his music is linear. Organum of fifths and fourths from the earliest polyphonic era is retained along with a few established forms and to this is added the large contemporary vocabulary.

His linear technique includes contrapuntal movement with consonant harmonies resulting, but more often smoothly shaven dissonant harmonies are the outcome:

Ex. 35. Second String Quartet (Passacaglia)

In multi-voice counterpoint clarity is the prime requisite. Schuman may blend a principal voice with a second, a third with a fourth, and a fifth with a sixth. Then the three groups of paired voices are combined in **six-part counterpoint**. This interlocking of voices produces a characteristically dissonant effect while preserving clarity of texture.

Two-part counterpoint is enriched by octave-coupling. In *Requiescat* the voices hum throughout, moving mostly in unison and two-part coupling:

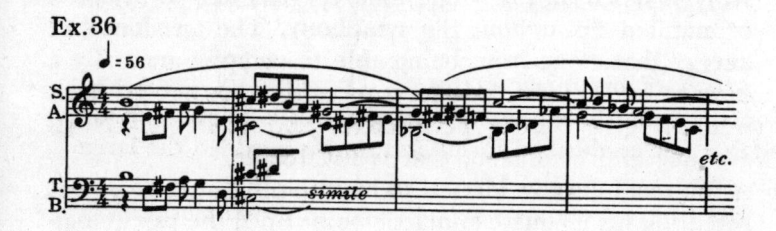

Ex. 36

Form Ideas

Schuman thinks in long-range terms, plotting the course of a large-scale work before the writing actually begins. Germinal ideas are chosen for their emotional power; then they are sorted and studied carefully for their potentialities and run a first-rate obstacle course trying to break through his musical thought processes. The material selected takes form as a more or less complete organism before reaching paper. A thematic idea is seldom used unless a detailed plan of the entire work can be laid upon it. A picture of the future must be there. The possible sonorities of the medium are weighed and tested for properties in relation to the initial material. Occasionally, certain aspects of the music are sketched in rough. A kind of "dummy" music is written to get the feel of the piece.

Schuman's faculty for self criticism keeps him on the alert for bad spots. His ability to seek out beforehand the places where the music will falter, and either alter the original theme or nonchalantly throw it out, saves him many futile pages. Pieces do not have to be scrapped at the halfway mark because of irremovable defects. Hindsight has no place in the technique of composition.

It is during this process of blending form-ideas beforehand that astoundingly original things happen. This panoramic view enables Schuman to contrive unique structural schemes. His Second Symphony is a one-movement work integrated by a single predominating theme. The entire work is based on the single tone C. This tone is sounded or implied throughout the symphony. The freedom and energy that come from being able to compose mentally a passage leading to a coda for a piece that has not yet been written, give him a perspective, and consequently an architectural command, that is invaluable.

Schuman devotes himself to maintaining interest by not revealing his ultimate climactic point until the psychological moment for release comes. This suspense treatment precludes dangerous let-downs and carries even the uninitiated listener over strange and wildly imaginative passages with comparative ease.

The majority of works begin without introductions. Normally, introductions are used to establish a mood, to present material for further development, or to disclose a separate entity. These approaches hold little interest for Schuman. His initial ideas barge in intently and with impact. The Symphony for Strings, for example, begins suddenly and noisily with all the violins in unison:

Ex. 37

He usually uses introductions only when establishing a tonality for singers:

Ex. 38. *Holiday Song*

[musical example: Voice and Piano, ♩ = 100, "When was it ev-er a" etc.]

Up to about 1946 transitions gave Schuman trouble. They were either so important that they gave an impression of being independent sections, or so short that they formed a bridge too weak to link the sections. He had better luck when he forgot about lacing his sections and kept them moving until they grew into each other. Schuman soon realized this. His later music moves in long lines and grows from one idea to the next without the customary transitions. Characteristic figures resulting from the development of one section's material generate the thematic constituents of the next. Therefore, all elements that make up a piece are related to each other and form a tight structure, free of loose ends.

This approach insures uniformity of design and accounts for the clear shape of his long works. It leaves no room for impressionistic scattering of ideas, or annoying breaks that let in fickle cadenzas. No vague harmonies are needed to glaze a page spattered with odds and ends of themes. Program music as so often diseased by impressionistic formulas of the 20th century is alien to him. The few pieces that bear descriptive titles (with the sole exception of *Newsreel*) are translations of psychological states into tonal language.

The absence of literal recapitulation is characteristic of Schuman's writing as well as that of most of his contemporaries. Once he makes a statement he cannot reiterate unless it has experienced alteration. In the Piano Concerto (first movement) the returning principal theme brings with it material that grew out of the development of the movement. The new ideas are interwoven among the elements of the returning theme, which, in itself, is drastically altered. Its dimensions, structural make-up, instrumentation, and texture have changed. Only the general feeling remains, though gaining in energy and precision.

In later works, themes are often introduced almost simultaneously. The first movement of the Fourth String Quartet is primed by the second theme, which enters before the first theme is fully stated. In the Sixth Symphony there are three outstanding themes: the passacaglia, which remains unaltered during four statements; the A theme, which begins in the seventh measure, before the passacaglia theme completes one statement; and B, which joins A during the fourth passacaglia statement.

Orchestral Sense

Ideas occur to Schuman in their inherent instrumental setting. A theme is never given the schoolmaster's instrumentation test of being put through the paces of all instruments beforehand, to see if it can be played by everyone. It may grow and take on changing shapes. Each player who gets a whack at it finds that his version is constructed in a manner best suited to his instrument, yet the most virtuoso fugue theme is played by every instrument even though a player may have to share it with another member of his section.

Schuman is concerned with the possibilities rather than the limitations of instruments. This is a healthy attitude. One never feels that the composer hesitates or is doubtful. He knows what instruments are just able to do and builds passages that exploit such extremes. Music of this kind is bold and sharp, and sometimes terrifying. He will take chances. The tremendous effect obtained from four agile trumpets moving in four independent parts (in the Third Symphony) is that of an electric trumpet machine. By a clever manipulation of cross rhythms the fast runs keep up while the individual players have comfortable breathing spaces and well spaced runs:

Ex. 39. Third Symphony (Fugue)

One cannot miss Schuman's fondness for blocks of instrumental color. He thinks primarily in terms of three main choirs: strings, woodwinds, and brass. No one section is used as the backbone of the orchestra. Each has a feeling of virtuoso liberation. Schuman loves the band, especially when writing for orchestra. The pure full brass tone in the Third Symphony fugue is fresh, and a welcome relief from fast-moving *tutti:*

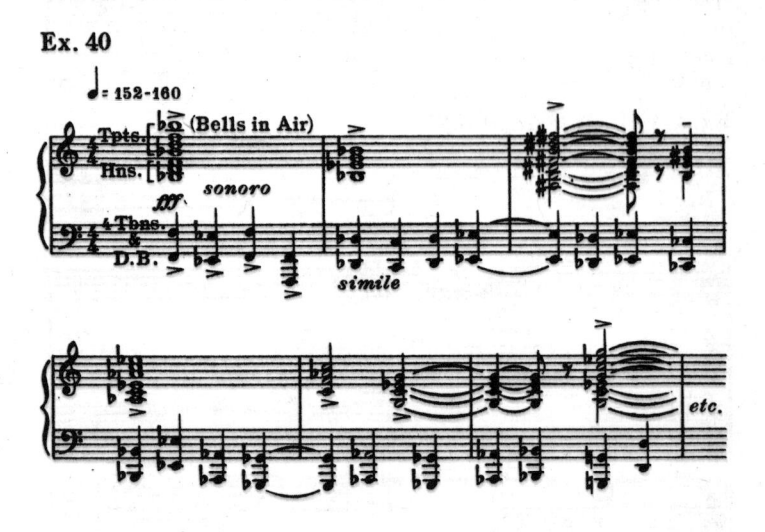

Ex. 40

Schuman's orchestra shines and full pages never sound muddled. Each instrumental group is contrapuntally and harmonically integrated. He knows how to space the brass to make the most of the natural overtones of a resonant chord, and understands that reinforcing declamatory brass with woodwinds rubs off the luster. Instead of doubling the fugal horn passage in the Third Symphony with bassoons, clarinets, and arco strings, as Richard Strauss might have done, Schuman gets more sound by preserving the horn luster. Pizzicato strings are added for punch. (See Ex. 81.)

Any device that will retain a musical idea in an easier form is worth consideration. Schuman is full of tricks that facilitate performance. He knows that it is safer to assume that his piece will be played with insufficient rehearsal. Difficult passages are divided between similar instruments whenever possible. Such division gives trumpets the freedom of an oboe and oboes the punch of a trumpet.

There are several marked characteristics in his orchestral coloring. Muted strings are not limited to soft and delicate playing. They sound like an additional string section when used as declaimers of intense passages:

Ex. 41. Third Symphony

He can scramble strings and preserve their clarity by coupling:

Ex. 42. Third Symphony

He is not confined to backboning the orchestra by strings and is not afraid to use brasses for soft background:

Ex. 43. *Undertow*

Schuman is fond of timpani solos:

Ex. 44. Sixth Symphony

and of fast unison woodwind passages in continuous motion:

Ex.45. Fourth Symphony

Vocal Style

In some respects Schuman's vocal music is simpler than his instrumental because a great deal of it was written for amateur chorus. It is true that in writing for a chorus of girls from Sarah Lawrence he was constrained to the use of a simpler harmonic and contrapuntal technique, but he realized that he did not have to hold back rhythmically. He managed to cover a wide gamut of feeling within the physical limitations of this medium. On the printed page numerous passages look too difficult rhythmically for the amateur. These complexities are born of the natural rhythms of jazz, so much a part of the American people. With intelligent training, amateurs can sing rhythmically complicated music. These rhythms are second nature to the large percentage of the untrained population. It is on this score that Robert Shaw and his groups took off for heights seldom scaled by semi-professional singers. It is on this premise that William Schuman set forth to write a choral literature challenging to the amateur and endearing to the professional, works that can well be treated as etudes in contemporary choral singing. They make a stilted small-town choral group supple, cut into the ice of a professionally stereotyped outfit, and widen the field for other composers.

Texts on democratic themes are preferred. The *Prelude for Voices* with words by Thomas Wolfe is not typical of Schuman's choice of text. Introspection of the type represented by such a line as: "Which of us is not forever a stranger and alone?" is seldom found in his choral works:

Ex. 46

[musical example: Sop. Solo — "Which of us is not for-ev-er a stran-ger and a-lone?" (Chorus on "Mm")]

Whitman or the Whitmanesque lines of Genevieve Taggard are more usual. Lines on the destiny of American folk attract Schuman. He creates as one of the folk, yet avoids quotation; he can handle a patriotic theme without burlesque or nausea.

Schuman sets English to melody without falsifying the natural rhythm of the language. When music and words want to take different paths he usually gives in to the words. Form and melodic line are determined by the text and the musical rhythm is guided by speech rhythm:

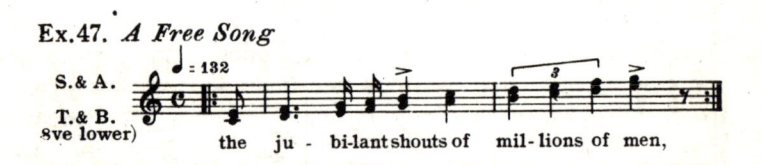

Ex. 47. *A Free Song*

[musical example: S. & A., T. & B. (8ve lower) — "the ju-bi-lant shouts of mil-lions of men,"]

The mood of the text strongly determines the harmonic texture and background patterns. Musical illustration is secondary to the verbal setting, yet the finished product entails no sacrifice of musical freedom:

Ex. 48. *Prologue*

Schuman can twist voice parts unmercifully and still they will "sound". Without a change of harmony he can create excitement solely from his rhythmic resources:

Ex. 49. *A Free Song*

(musical score: SATB, ♩ = 132, text: "song, a new song, a free song, a new...")

His voices move freely in canonic passages, avoiding harmonic snags. He may content himself with no harmonic movement, but never with interrupted harmonic movement (the plague of canons):

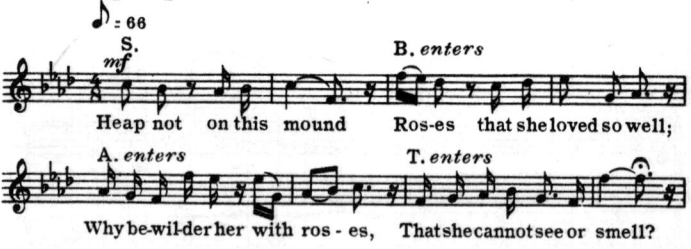

Ex. 50. *Epitaph* from Four Canonic Choruses

(musical score: ♪ = 66, mf, with entries S., A., B., T.; text: "Heap not on this mound Roses that she loved so well; Why bewilder her with ros-es, That she cannot see or smell?")

Schuman considers recitative less powerful than straight song, and avoids it. He must have power, even if he is compelled to use long unison passages or coupled two-part counterpoint to get it. The *a cappella*, eight-part chorus,

Pioneers!, opens with coupled two-part counterpoint using all voices. Later, it spreads into rich eight-part writing:

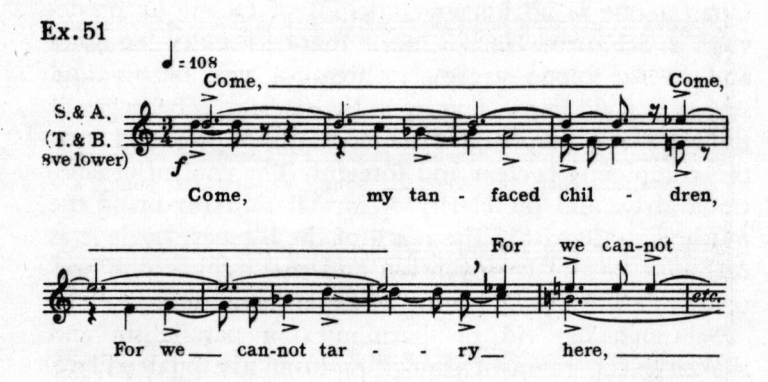

Ex. 51

None of his style traits are lost while writing for chorus. This music is less intricate than the symphonies but retains the essence of the larger works. The piece called Choral Etude has a shifting tonal plan no less subtle than a layout of a chamber work. Notice the consecutives in the opening of the Choral Etude. Not even singers can frighten Schuman away from consecutive fifths:

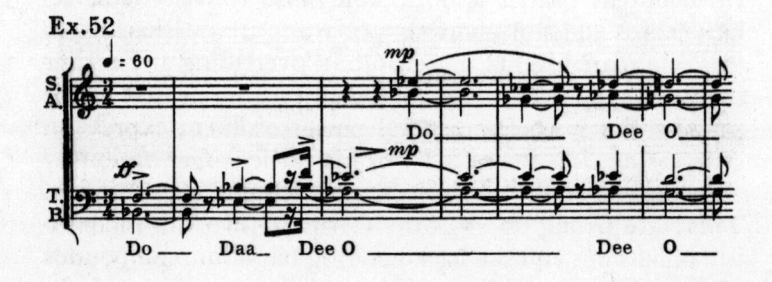

Ex. 52

New Directions

In the Sixth Symphony, *Judith,* and the Fourth String Quartet one is no longer conscious of technique or devices in Schuman. Here is music that gets under the notes and in the blood stream. It breathes lyric beauty and stamps a vivid impression upon the listener. The pages of the scores are complex but the music that is projected from this complexity is clear and forceful. The control of emotional drive and the clarity of formal thinking bring the music directly within the reach of the listener. Logic is at no point outrun by invention and the architectural pattern is devoid of any feeling of experimentation.

Schuman has rid his harmonies of parallelism and shaken excess resonant sonorities from his tonal palette. Inner voices have become active and sectionalism is no longer a stumbling block. His bass part has grown strong and now dictates harmonic progressions resulting in a new chromatic-melodic admixture. These recently acquired procedures mark clearly a growth in formal conception, harmonic imagination, and thematic scope in the later Schuman.

His widening harmonic palette includes a chromaticism that can be traced to his First Symphony, for an urge to carry on with certain elements that were unquestionably ruled out by Harris is noticeable. The Harris triadic relationships and polychordal specialties are no shackles to this Schuman. He has no scruple in overriding any earlier theory for the sake of an ecstatic chromaticism that might interest him now. His general power of fluent expression grows as he risks the security of his earlier organization by allowing elements of American eclecticism to seep through. There are strong traces of the German-American modernism of Sessions and the back-bending harmonic compounds of Ives. He is gambling wisely as he sets out to enlarge his rhetorical scope.

Each new piece brings forth more new harmonic elements and *Voyage,* a cycle of five piano pieces, for example, uncovers fantastic shapes and crevices. There is less preoccupation with open confession and good health, as cringing gestures are veiled by complex harmonic textures that have been soaked in the chromatic liquor of the Fourth String Quartet. A touch of personal shyness is present in the late works while climactic points are approached cautiously and one section is never completely freed from the shadow of another. In the Sixth Symphony the fast music is under constant surveillance of the slow music, and in the light but straight and serious *Casey*, no one of the many short pieces ever completely rids itself of the contact made with the previous number. The elements of comedy and pathos rub so hard they fuse into a hot "freeze" —the tableaux of fans and players.

The heroic dualism caused by the resistance of the diatonic to the chromatic in the Sixth Symphony, the personal passion and violence of *Voyage,* and the spastic muscles bound tight by *Judith's* chromatic lines, point to the new directions in Schuman's music. Though seeking new soils this composer's musical personality never pales, for the foundation of his musical grammar remains based upon the principles of vocal harmony, and his musical rhetoric, upon such phenomena as the emotional effect of top notes or gutteral sounds in the human voice. The ability to deliver an entire sentence without interruption before taking apart its pregnant clauses has been his from the beginning. This sure technique enables Schuman to concentrate on a specific idea, regardless of new materials used, without digressing. The strength of his specific expressivity and dramatic conception will serve him well in his constant search for abstract perfection.

* * *

This is William Schuman's craft. In discussing it we have uncovered a cross-section of his entire output. However, a more thorough and detailed analysis of a few works that are easily available in score or on records may give us a better understanding and taste of his music. We shall begin with a representative early work, the *American Festival Overture*.

AMERICAN FESTIVAL OVERTURE

The *American Festival Overture* is an excellent example of motif growth and melodic invention because it is built entirely on a three-note germinal idea and its subsequent alterations. Schuman wanted to write for the occasion music that stemmed directly from the American idiom; he probably wanted to write a piece and summon a public at the same time. So he chose as the nucleus for his overture the street-cry "Wee-Awk-Eee", familiar to him from his boyhood days in New York and known among city youngsters as a call to play.

Schuman is not the only composer to use this motif. It has become the symbol of exultation and triumph in American music. Copland uses it with brasses for his personalized and bony *tutti*. Harris likes it in triple-*forte,* muted string declamations. Barber harmonizes it in logical part-writing. Sessions hides it and Virgil Thomson adores it. The motif, whether written in major or minor, Locrian or Lydian, looks like this:

Ex. 53

After passing through Schuman's restless spine it takes the following shape in the opening measure of the overture:

Ex. 54

He solves the modal and harmonic texture problem by a unison statement.

And now all time-honored alteration devices enter. Two important versions of the motif emerge. Version No. 1, an enlargement of the motif, appears in the sixth measure with chromatics:

Ex. 55

Right on its heels comes an exhilarating augmentation:

Ex. 56

which is tickled into spurting out the last four chromatic notes in diminution. The tempo is fast, yet the second important version of the motif occurs in the twelfth measure with strings:

Ex. 57

The resultant interval of the fourth becomes increasingly important. The last tied note in the example above continues with a phrase that contains an inversion of the call to play, "Awk-Wee-Awk!"

Ex. 58

All this happens in barely a dozen measures. The uninitiated listener got lost at the third eighth of the ninth measure (first note of Ex. 56); easy-going ears called it the third beat and followed through having a wonderful time. Everyone can catch up on the Victor disk. This is a typical Schuman opening—no introductory fanning, no shuffling for excitement, but a charge straight to the point made with unstinted drive.

In measure 17, the melodic fourth motif becomes the brass harmony (Schuman's first harmonic commitment). Over and under the chord is found dismemberment of the theme:

Ex. 59

The next passage is the wildest kind of imitation. It is dangerously scored for rotating choirs of strings, brass, and high and low woodwinds. Each instrumental group gets to play only two-note fragments:

Ex. 60

Str.　　Brass　W.W.　　W.W.　Str.　　W.W.

In the midst of this extensive imitation the initial minor-third motif is expanded to a major third and augmented fourth. A rhythmic figure coinciding with the fundamental beat stands firmly under this erratic alteration of the melody:

Ex. 61

The "call to play" motif is hurried rhythmically:

Ex. 62 Brass

and

Ex. 63 Strings

to prepare for a stream of full unison woodwinds that present version No. 1 (Ex. 55) of the motif in lively sixteenth notes:

Ex. 64

The theme is now stretched almost to the breaking point by interval expansion:

Ex. 65

Solo timpani keep the section from getting out of hand by slowing down the motif with rhythmic alteration:

Ex. 66

This leads to a weak transition consisting solely of F-sharps. Here the composer seems stunned. He gasps for breath and regains it too soon. The slow section is extremely short. Yet it presents a free inversion of version No. 1 which is so hauntingly beautiful that one almost forgives the skimpy dimensions:

Ex. 67

Eng. Horn (Ob. an 8ve higher)

A pseudo-canonic treatment brings in the trumpet and flute in octaves with a partial statement of the inversion:

Ex. 68

Schuman's tendency at the time this work was written, to overuse chords built by fourths, had no ill-effects on this overture. The predominance of chords by fourths is justifiable because of the implication of the second version of the motif (Ex. 57). The interval of the fourth is significant enough melodically to warrant its presence in the prevailing harmonic scheme. In the following fugal section the fourth becomes increasingly important as it is used to reach the peak in the theme's second measure. This fugue subject contains every melodic alteration presented in the previous sections. The short exclamations unite into one impelling statement which forms the core of the piece:

Ex. 69

The fugue moves ahead, undisturbed by an ingenious chorale that slips in before the fourth entry of the subject. An inversion of the motif is sung by the violas with the characteristic interval both contracted and augmented for quiet contrast:

Ex. 70

dolce cantabile

The entire exposition is handled by the strings while the woodwinds take on the burden of the development. This use of pure orchestral choirs is inevitable in a Schuman work. When the strings reappear they expose a liquid and strict canon built directly on the chorale. Meanwhile the woodwinds break up the fugue and juggle its parts. The coda brings in the brass, which have played no part in the fugue. Their function is to present the motif in augmentation and take bearings as though a strict recapitulation were in store:

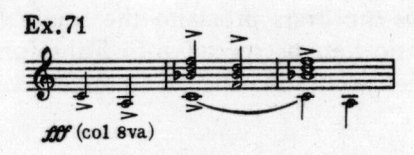

Ex. 71

fff (col 8va)

The final section is recapitulatory in that it crystallizes the opening section and settles the dispute between two prominent versions of the motif (the scale-wise figure and the interval of the fourth). Both elements are presented in diminution (the first also in retrogression):

Ex. 72

The melodic fourth holds out longer and grows into huge chords by fourths over insistent underlying rhythms:

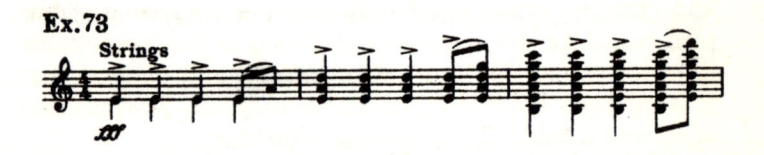

Ex. 73

Around this harmonic mass revolves much of the initial material, and in the final *tutti* passage the strings play a nervous contraction of the motif:

Ex. 74

Against this the brass proclaim the original motif while the harmonic fourths spread into fifths forming a rock-bottom cadence culminating on a polychord.

The Third Symphony

The vigorous Third Symphony is the most brilliantly written work of Schuman's early period. A robust athleticism has built its unique architecture; its virility extends even to the lyricism, which is strong and nonsubjective.

The symphony is divided into two parts with two connected movements in each: Passacaglia and Fugue, and Chorale and Toccata. Passacaglias, canons, and fugues appear in many of Schuman's works. So far as he is concerned the possibilities of older forms have not been thoroughly explored. The essence of these forms is the thing that attracts him, and while he employs many of the standard devices, the manner in which they are developed and changed under his hands causes a surprisingly new plan to evolve. He regards these forms as natural foundations for supporting musical organisms, and believes that if freed from contrapuntal artifice they can be fresh and alive, and worthy of any musical expression.

The Fugue is a set of free variations on its canonic opening, which is derived from the Passacaglia theme; and the Passacaglia is a linear prelude to the Fugue. The entire work is based upon the Passacaglia theme and a remarkably unified whole is achieved. The most important features of the theme are its salient intervallic traits. The violas state the theme:

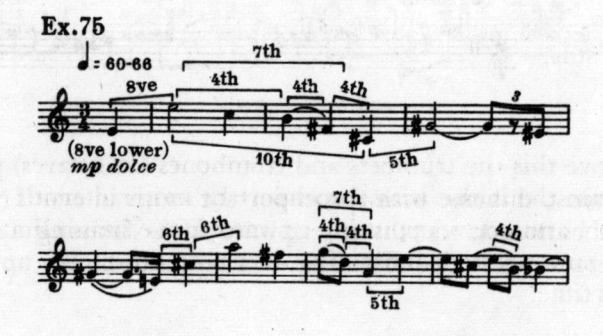

Ex. 75

These melodic characteristics form the basis of the entire thematic structure of the symphony, and are prominent in the detailed development of each movement. Among the distinguishing qualities of the theme are the octave leaps; the fourths combining to form a seventh; the rising sixths and fifths; and the falling over-all tenth at the beginning.

The viola statement on E is followed canonically (on rising semitones to B-flat) by entrances of the second violins, 'cellos, first violins, double basses with low woodwinds, horns, and high woodwinds. These seven entrances unfold a strict four-part canon and avoid a seven-voice structure. When the violas, second violins, and 'cellos reach the end of their canonic line they jump to the aid of the winds with a clarifying pizzicato reinforcement. This doubling insures that there are never more than four contrapuntal voices. As the instruments pile up on rising semitones, the symphony gains force quickly. Accompanying counterpoint adds to the tense opening by employing the melodic features of the theme in diminution. The climbing octave and occasional fifth reaching for a firmer grip dominate the counterpoint. At relaxed places, descending fourths enable the multi-moving lines to breathe.

Variation I (50th measure) begins with a background of consistent harmonic and rhythmic texture. It engages the octave motif in ornamental play:

Ex. 76

Above this the trumpets and trombones (in octaves) paraphrase the theme with the important motif intervals (fifth, sixth, and octave) pointing upward to the brass climax on the trumpet high B-flat. The over-all tenth moves upward this time:

Ex. 77

10th

A transitional brass passage forces the melodic fourth downward and prepares it for pulverization by hammered polychords in the following variation. This transition employs full brass except tuba. The burden of supplying the entire brass section with a bottom tone is taken by the fourth trombone. This gives the chords smack and tang.

Triad harmony used so far is suddenly taken over by polychords of intense and savage character. They form the groundwork of Variation II. The strings, low woodwinds, tuba, and timpani insist on repeating the polychordal formations in rhythms related to a fragment (mm. 3 and 4) of the theme (Ex. 75). The remaining woodwinds give out the last cries of this growing exclamation in an effective asthmatic wheeze (a melodic variation of the theme):

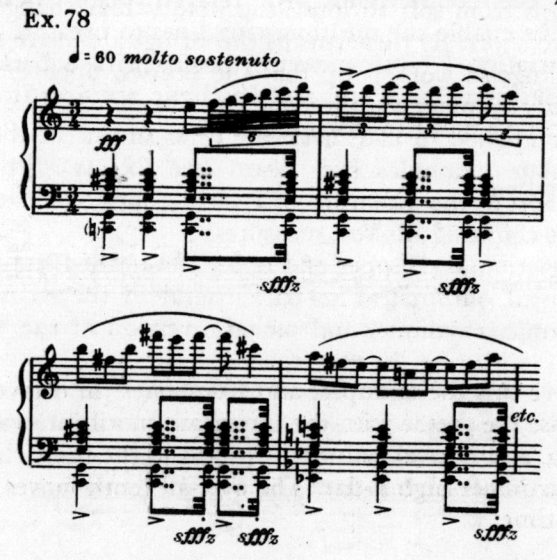

Ex. 78

An eleven-measure transition slows down the dynamo by augmenting the material of the preceding second variation. From the commotion of ornamenting the thematic characteristics, a new interval—the second—has become important. This interval is used as a quieting influence on the next variation.

Variation III is a long melodic version of the theme carried by the violins in octaves while the 'cellos murmur continuous sixteenth notes:

Ex. 79

The variation begins quietly and prepares for the second ingenious crescendo of the work. While the dynamics progress from soft to loud, the note values change from long to short. By these means the strings alone are able to get things so worked up that the brasses, upon entering, can only stammer out three measures of chords. The strings are compelled to take back the reins in one of the most articulate scrambles ever heard (see Ex. 42). This spot can capture the attention of even the most routined timpanist counting his rest measures.

Variation IV is sober and tight, and headed straight for the fugal outburst. The background in the strings is a harmonic, rhythmic, and melodic version of the theme's characteristics set in even rows:

Ex. 80

Under this consistent rhythm four trombones give the final summary of the Passacaglia in four-part harmony. Throughout the variation the trombones and strings (without double basses) proceed unmolested by other instruments.

Without an irritating retard or a rupturing cadence the Fugue subject makes a dramatic entrance. It comes in with gigantic boldness and strength. Four horns reinforced by pizzicato violas and 'cellos give it punch:

Ex. 81

The subject is related in design to the Passacaglia theme but is of different rhythmic nature. It uses precisely the same intervals. The leap of the octave gains strength by beginning on the strong beat and assumes new character by reversing its direction. The interval of the tenth is spanned in a measure and a half and Schuman regains the original register by turning the octave upward again. The hidden thirds of the Passacaglia now emerge in the last measure of the Fugue subject. Schuman's melodic thirds become minor and accented when approaching the triumphant. It is on this motif that the entire symphony ultimately reaches its peak.

The subject entrances on rising semitones from B-flat through E reflect the Passacaglia opening, where voices entered on rising semitones from E to B-flat. The Fugue runs into seven parts through canonic development. There is a three and a half-measure codetta after each four-measure subject entry except the first. This throws the initial beat of each entry alternately on the first and second half of the measure. The sequence of answers is as follows:

violins on B, violas and 'cellos on C, tuba and pizzicato basses on D-flat, woodwinds on D, trombones on E-flat, and trumpets on E. Since no parts drop out, seven voices accumulate. This is complex orchestral writing and yet the seven-part counterpoint is clear and clean.

An extended episode follows. Four high trumpets play a fast canonic contraction of the subject with the facility of a keyboard instrument (see Ex. 39). A quieting transition with the unaccompanied English horn leading prepares for a variation of the Fugue. This section is concerned with the embellishment of the downward octave by woodwinds and strings:

Ex. 82

The eighth-note figure is eventually joined by the muted strings in a triangular garb of long singing tones. Climaxing the variation, a timpani solo introduces the dotted rhythm in one measure of the Fugue subject (stemming directly from the Passacaglia theme) that forms the basis of the second variation of the Fugue:

Ex. 83

The timpani engage the strings in a furious rhythmic battle. Brasses punch long-held notes, each ending with the dotted-note figure. From this point on to the end the music pushes forward relentlessly.

In the final section there are three elements: an ornamented pedal-point around E-flat (derived from the preceding variation), melodic dialogue between the trombones and horns (from the pedal-point turns), and a dialogue between the woodwinds and strings on a new variation of the subject. These elements worked together formulate a vigorous *tutti*. Just before the end a huge brass band sounds off the Fugue subject in irregular augmentation against the first variation's embellished octave (see Ex. 40).

Part II opens with a Chorale derived from the Passacaglia theme. Violas and 'cellos divided begin molding the shape of the chorale melody. The chorale proper is sung by a solo trumpet:

Ex. 84

As in the Fugue, the falling over-all tenth is picked up by the rising octave, thereby regaining the original register. In measure three, the tenth is inverted to prepare for the high G hold. Again, fourths combine to form the characteristic interval of the seventh.

The solo flute carries the trumpet line up into its own highest register, then drops gradually to form a luminous arc of light. As the flute falls out of sight a harmonic string background takes over. Descending melodic fourths direct the strings to a variant of the chorale. Embellishment resulting in melodic seconds produces an inversion of the Fugue's first variation. Second violins and violas unfold free diminution of the figure the first violins and 'cellos are playing:

Ex. 85

A sudden crescendo brings a loud but hollow sounding chorale statement in two bare lines played by the woodwinds and strings. In coupled two-part counterpoint, four horns wend their way (via the melodic second) down to a dark close. Divided violas and 'cellos waver on the interval of the second and soon nothing is left but the bassoons' lowest B-flats.

The Toccata begins while the low B-flats are held. The complete rhythm of the principal theme (fourteen measures) is taken by a quiet snare drum. Then the bass clarinet exposes the melodic contour of the theme while the snare intersperses comments:

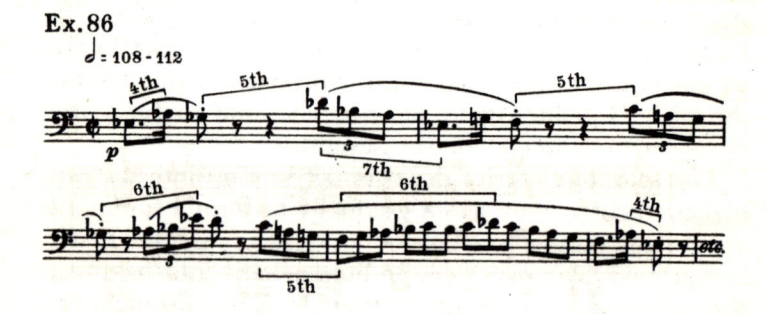

Ex. 86

The Toccata is a display piece full of virtuoso passages for solo instruments and groups of instruments, and each player is challenged by the thematic material. The intervallic structure of the melody is derived from the Passacaglia; the octave characteristic is held back until its release in the ninth measure. The bass clarinet runs from its lowest E-flat up three octaves to its highest E-flat, swoops down, and involves all the woodwinds in a wild game. As in Part I, the voices enter canonically. Each member of the woodwinds is compelled to try the theme. When the oboe cannot make the swoop the piccolo helps out. The total effect is one of extreme brilliance and speed, with a bustle of buzzes and shrieks.

The oboe tries singing the bass-clarinet tune in long notes,

Ex. 87

but the rest soon crowd him out. A short transition leads to a cadenza section for all the strings where the first variation of the Fugue is given a workout.

The closing sections continue to bring the symphony's material together. The Chorale is given a rhythmic massage:

Ex. 88

The Toccata theme is augmented against the dialogue material of the final section of the Fugue:

Ex. 89

[musical notation: Strings / Muted Brass]

Rhythmic blocks from the Passacaglia's first variation are inserted:

Ex. 90

[musical notation]

and the resultant minor-third motif from the Passacaglia development is shouted by the brass while the remaining choirs drum out the underlying Toccata rhythms.

Symphony for Strings

The Symphony for Strings nearly bursts with tunes. These are embedded in the formal structure and are set forth in the most brilliant string writing. The Larghissimo, in its expressive dignity, is encompassed by a bombastic opening movement and a finale that scurries impulsively.

The predominating polyphony of the first movement is prepared by an incisive A theme, torn open by *fortissimo* violins in unison. Four melodic elements in the theme are vital to the entire first movement:

Ex. 91

[Musical notation: Molto agitato ed energico ♩.=76, showing Element No.1, Expansion of No.1, Element No.2, Element No.3 (from No.1), Alteration of No.2, Element No.4 (closing figure)]

This twelve-measure subject pushes and jabs its way over a range of more than two octaves, while the dotted-half beat is split three ways,

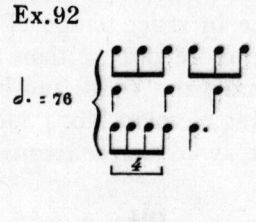

Ex. 92

[Musical notation: ♩.=76]

each rhythmic pattern making its way as one of the melodic elements. The widely spanned A theme enters three times to form the whole of section A.

The violas and 'cellos join in the second entry of the theme with a transformation of element No. 2,

Ex. 93

while the implied harmony of the theme's eighth and ninth measures becomes reality in pliable chordal textures:

Ex. 94

The direction of the A theme entering for the second time differs from that of the first in that the very end is dominated by an inversion of element No. 1 that proves important to the progress of the work:

Ex. 95

The third entrance of the theme employs all the instruments, but this time the 'cellos and basses are dared to play the difficult A theme in strict tempo. The harmonies in the upper voices are more intense than those in the preceding entry, and finally the 'cellos and basses turn in the direction of the closing element No. 4 and strip it of ornaments just in time to avoid a treacherous descent.

Theme B is built on A's element No. 3, scraped clean of ornaments. The violas sound even louder without the violins over their heads, and the three rhythmic divisions of the fundamental beat (see Ex. 92) are thoroughly shuffled. B is a straightforward statement of element No. 3 grafted to the inversion of element No. 1 (Ex. 95):

Ex. 96

The triplet rhythmic figure finally rids itself of the other two figures and a polychordal development section breaks in. The development is concerned solely with the inversion of element No. 1, which had not been exploited to the same extent as the other elements:

Ex. 97

A development section that is built entirely on the initial theme's opening motif (element No. 1) cannot be followed by a recapitulation that opens with the same motif. Therefore Schuman begins the returning A theme at its eighth measure. However, after only three measures there is no development aftertaste and the basses surprise the violins with a complete statement of A. This movement's vigorous motion has not let up so far and now it is too late, so more notes than the exposition had led us to expect are added. Theme B (incorporating element No. 1 inverted) looks like this in the recapitulation:

Ex. 98

To balance matters, the coda is imbedded in the harmonic texture of the development section. Then the melodic third of the A theme's third measure attempts to drive the piece, which has been dominated by melodic seconds, to a "Wee-Awk-Eee" close,

Ex. 99

but the strings organize to declaim the first measure of the symphony and put an end to the issue (see Ex. 29).

The Larghissimo movement is a restrained and mature example of Schuman's writing. The material is presented on two horizontal planes: first, the groundwork is laid by broad and muted chords (see Ex. 13), then the opening melody sings above, forming a fifteen-measure arc:

Ex. 100

The melodic outline of the harmonic pattern below forms, by inversion, a long canon beginning at measure 19:

Ex. 101

The canonic answer appears twelve measures later, where above it, counterpoint No. 1 takes the shape of the opening groundwork (which equals the inversion of the canon theme):

Ex. 102

At the second canonic answer, counterpoint No. 2 alters the canon theme, so that now three versions of the introduction's profile are being stated at once:

Ex. 103

Throughout the canon, the low strings pluck half-note chords patiently until the violas pick up the very last melodic turn of the canon and lead others in a sixteenth-note figure that bolsters the canon melody. The melodic line and the sixteenth-note lines are coupled,

Ex. 104

and extended to a climax of broad chords (strings without mutes) derived from the opening of the movement. The close reverts to both elements of the first part, the introductory harmonic pattern and the melody above, and subsides to *pianississimo* triads.

The lively finale (Presto) is in rondo form and the theme is varied at each appearance. Although in its course it becomes sustained, the basic tempo is not relaxed. The exhilarating A theme (see Ex. 8) is preoccupied with melodic seconds (similar to those used in the first movement). B, too, slaps seconds carelessly in a pizzicato free-for-all:

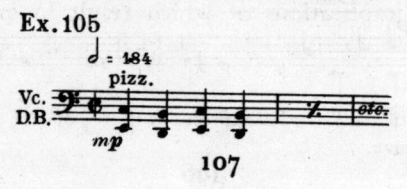

Ex. 105

This pizzicato section is not a "spontaneous paraphrase of the Tchaikovsky Fourth"[1] but its superficial resemblance can mislead a gullible listener. The return of A leads to sustained chords that prepare for a quiet and melodic C theme which is contrived from a retrogression of A's first measure:

Ex. 106

This section, a canon, grows in complexity through the statement of seven voices and returns to A in martial augmentation. As C and A become involved, the bass part of the original A comes to the fore in a bright *ostinato* which cues in the coda. A variant of A in triplets hops over the *ostinato*, causing a staggering of rhythms not unlike those of the first movement, until the D-major tonic stamps and pounds for the remaining twelve measures.

UNDERTOW (CHOREOGRAPHIC EPISODES FOR ORCHESTRA)

William Schuman's forty-minute ballet, *Undertow*, is one of the serious dances in the Ballet Theatre repertory. The composer and Antony Tudor, choreographer of *Undertow*, have prepared the following summary of the ballet:

> The ballet for which this score was composed concerns itself with the emotional development of a transgressor. The choreographic action depicts a series of related happenings, the psychological implications of which result in an inevitable murder.

---

[1] As the notes in the record album put it.

The hero is seen at various stages, beginning with his babyhood when he is neglected by his mother who leaves him hungry while she seeks the embrace of her husband. The frustrations engendered by this episode are heightened during boyhood and adolescence by his sordid experiences in the lower reaches of a large city. He encounters prostitutes, street-urchins, an innocent young girl, a gay bridal couple, carousing dipsomaniacs, and a visiting mission worker whose friendship and care he seeks.

The emotions aroused in the abnormal youth by these episodes—revulsion, rage, terror, loneliness, fear of domination—result in climax after climax, reaching a peak in his murder of a lascivious woman.

It is only when he is apprehended for this crime that his soul is purged by the tremendous relief that is his at the realization that he will no longer be called upon to endure the anguish of being a misfit and an outcast among his fellow men.

While originally the music served the action on the stage, Schuman's concert version succeeds in shaping it for symphonic requirements independent of the ballet. He contracted the music with such ingenuity that a completely new form evolved. This version stands on its own merits and will therefore be analyzed from a purely musical standpoint devoid of choreographic connotations.

The large orchestra employed is used sparingly; instruments are rarely doubled and *tutti* are scarce. The entire opening section uses only three chords. The first is quiet and long in duration but eventually the second and third are unearthed explosively. The first chord is repeated eighteen times before the second fires in:

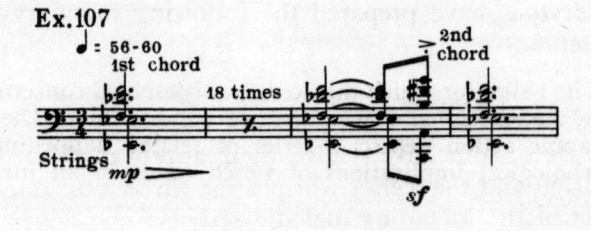

Ex.107

Six measures later, the third chord joins:

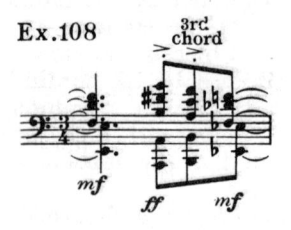

Ex. 108

Above these string chords, seeds for future thematic material are sown. The oboe and clarinet discuss the possibility of roosting on E-flat or E-natural:

Ex. 109

The bassoon tries C and the flute F-sharp, and soon they become tangled. In the B part of this first section (Tranquillo) unison strings free them and expose a simple solution to their problems:

Ex. 110

By the time the section closes, the bassoon, clarinet, oboe, and flute, respectively, give their approval of the string solution and the 'cellos whisper the three most important notes of the foregoing melodic activity:

Ex. 111

[musical notation: ♩ = 60, 3: note close — I, mp]

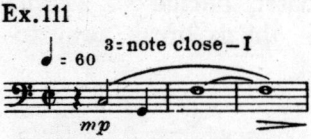

There is little hesitation from here on. One theme grows into another until four clear-cut ideas (aside from the introductory motifs) are set forth. The melodic contour of Theme No. 1 results from the note-quarreling in the introductory section and its rhythmic nervousness is evidence of the sporadic chordal rhythms of the opening:

Ex. 112. Theme No. 1
Leggero (♩ = 138)

[musical notation: Vc. ... Bn. ... mp ... etc.]

The passing notes of Theme No. 1 spread to the harmonic body, and a passing-chord figure, which beckons Theme No. 2, emerges. No. 1 is imitated rhythmically and melodically by the new theme:

Ex. 113. Theme No. 2
Più mosso
W.W. & Piano

[musical notation: Vlns. ... mf ... etc.]

A few measures later, Theme No. 2 clutches a motif whose active intervallic thirds break away to form their own theme (No. 3):

Ex. 114

The 'cellos test the strength of Theme No. 1 once more, but the bassoon brings up the topic of introductory heritage with a second three-note close, the first having been stated by the 'cellos:

Ex. 115

And before the delightful fourth theme can be sworn in, a series of recollections concur, beginning in measure 145 (B of the introduction, rhythmic twitches from Theme No. 1, and finally the whispering three-note close):

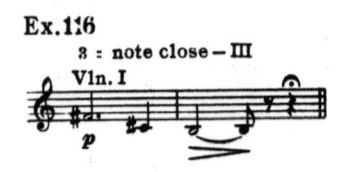

Ex. 116

Theme No. 4 ("like street-corner hymn singing") paraphrases the 'cello closing figure (Ex. 111) on the lap of Theme No. 3 (see Ex. 114). This "hymn" appears three times (see Exx. 17, 18, and 19) but between the statements lodge two huge developments of preceding material. Of particular importance is a new version of Theme No. 1 in Development I. Its new melodic sweep directs attention to a broad two-voice string canon in Development II while the winds brush away derived fragments. A long-awaited but short *tutti* gives the ensuing "religioso" statement (No. 3) of the "hymn" an almost repentant air.

The concluding section (measure 445) recapitulates the introductory music. The opening section's B part is stretched out over a rhythmic version of the A part. This material is noticeably colored by the experiences encountered in creating the themes of *Undertow*. While Theme No. 1 antagonizes this recapitulatory music that has begun to surge, a prolonged and dramatic peak is reached. The piano holds a frightening tone-cluster as the orchestra cuts off and the woodwinds try fleeing but are caught on a trill. After an alarming rim shot, percussions and lower strings utter spasmodic *pianissimi* and *fortissimi*. As the tension is held, brasses dissect the three chords of the introduction but the climactic passage disintegrates as a fragment of Theme No. 1 opposes the underground of Theme No. 2. The piece settles down on the original chord —this time held, repeated, or implied for thirty-six measures—while bells sound the melodic high points of the introductory section. *Undertow* ends quietly on a surprise chord, the tonic, whose identity (D-flat) has been withheld until the end. A few overtones linger until the 'cellos and basses gently press a low, single D-flat.

JUDITH

Schuman was confronted with an entirely new set of compositional problems in the Violin Concerto. The opening violin tune contained bold leaps that placed great demands on the supporting harmonies (see Ex. 9). As it progressèd, undulating harmonies and moving inner parts were necessary. Parallelism had to be pried loose from the harmonies, and resonant sonorities split open by boulders of intensely dissonant sounds. The active inner voices refused to stop short to make way for sectionalism and the bass voice grew strong and dictated the harmonies. Schuman was occupied with interlocking, extending, and bridging the sections and keeping his head above the pool of harmonic material created by the chromatic melodic admixture. These enigmatic problems presented formidable difficulties to him. The Sixth Symphony, *Judith,* and the Fourth String Quartet followed the Concerto and they show clearly the growth in formal conception, harmonic imagination, and thematic scope of this period. An analysis of *Judith,* a work that is well established in the new style-period, serves to point out this direction in which Schuman is working.

After Schuman's collaboration with Martha Graham on *Night Journey* he expressed the opinion that he "had long been convinced that modern dance suffers from the insufficient tonal resources its limited budgets permit. For this reason the music for modern choreography often sounds inadequate and places modern dance at a disadvantage when compared with the musical resources usually available to ballet companies." When the Louisville Philharmonic Society commissioned Martha Graham to create and perform a solo dance and to choose a composer, William Schuman was her selection and *Judith* the end result. The first performance took place on January 4, 1950, in Louisville, Kentucky, with Robert Whitney conducting. The ovation given the work in Louisville, and later in New York, made certain the survival of a new form—"concerto" for dancer and orchestra. This idea might well be adopted by dancers and composers and result in a new outlet for music and dance.

The story of *Judith* is part of the Apocryphal writings. It tells

Of how . . .
"Holofernes took the waters and the fountains of waters of the children of Israel . . . therefore, their young children were out of heart and their women and young men fainted of thirst. . . . and there was no longer any strength in them . . . and they were brought very low in the city . . ."

Of how . . .
"Judith fell upon her face . . . and cried with loud voice and said . . .
'O Lord God of my father Simeon to whom thou gavest a sword to take vengeance of the strangers . . . Give into mine hand the . . . power I have conceived . . .
Smite them by the deceit of my lips . . .
Break down their stateliness by the hand of a woman.
Lord God of the Heavens and Earth
Creator of the waters . . .
Hear my prayer.'"

Of how . . .
"Judith put off the garments of her widowhood for the exaltation of those that were oppressed."
and
"put on her garments of gladness . . . her bracelets and her chains and her ornaments . . ."

Of how . . .
"Judith went . . . down the mountain . . . to the tent of Holofernes . . ."

Of how . . .
"She abode in the camp three days . . . and she besought the Lord God to direct her way . . ."

Of how . . .
"On the fourth day Holofernes made a feast . . .
When Judith came in and sat down, Holofernes his heart was ravished with her . . . and he drank more wine than he had drunk at any one day since he was born . . ."

Of how . . .
"When evening came his servants made haste to depart . . . and Judith was left alone in the tent and Holofernes lying along his bed for he was filled with wine . . ."

Of how . . .
> "Judith standing by his bed said in her heart: 'O Lord God of all power . . . strengthen me this day . . .'"

Of how . . .
> "She took his head from him . . . and went forth up the mountain . . . and said with a loud voice:
>> 'Behold the head of Holofernes . . . the Lord has smitten him by the hand of a woman . . . I will sing unto the Lord a new song.'"

Of how . . .
> "The women . . . made a dance among them for her . . . and she took branches in her hand . . . and she went before all the people in the dance."

*   *   *

This is the story of Judith. But the myth from which the story stems is much older. The story has its foundations in some ancient fertility rite or ritual of re-birth, in which the woman casts off the garments of mourning . . . symbolic of her isolation, and puts on her garments of gladness . . . symbolic of her femininity . . . thereby defeating the enemy . . . Death.[1]

This dramatic and mature work contains numerous episodes and outbursts that are tightly integrated by potent thematic material. The themes are introduced early in the work and never wait for each other to disrobe. One does not stand by while the other is exposed. On the contrary, the presence of two or three themes is usually felt. Tiny segments of thematic material are often used to press a point, and when a whole section is based on a few notes of a specific theme, the motif grows to resemble other themes in the work.

Another unifying device is the use of triads with a minor second above or below a member of the chord. All five sections of *Judith* are flavored with this sound. It is this kind of harmony that enables Schuman to move in and out of polychords freely. The rhythms of the various themes are just as flexible as the harmony and, in fact, are transferable. If a returning melodic idea is not supported by a harmonic variation, a rhythm of another tune will be

---
[1] Note in the published score.

employed. At no time does one feel that a phrase has been orchestrated. Schuman thinks out his ideas orchestrally. Coats of orchestral color are not applied to the score, because the music is conceived orchestrally in the first place. No section can be satisfactorily studied apart from the orchestra. A piano reduction of a Schuman score would prove to be the poorest in the literature.

Judith begins with an A major-minor chord that generates triads with a minor ninth or major seventh added below one of its chord members. A slow rhythmic and harmonic discussion of the melodic minor seconds (first three notes) of the six-note theme continues for ten long measures before the last three notes appear:

Ex. 117. A Theme

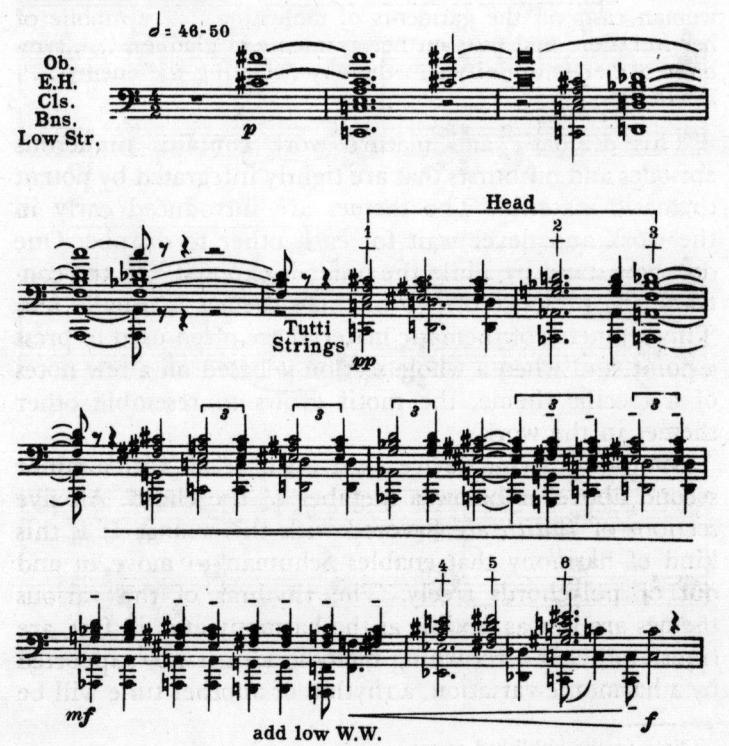

In the second phrase the six-note melody is extended and pushed up to where it duplicates the head of the tune, an octave higher. The initial A major-minor chord returns at this point and the brasses hammer the original chord in an effort to halt the chordal motion by repetition. Only two strong chords break through before the orchestra settles on a unison A, but the tension does not let up until the timpani silence the entire orchestra with the help of a stirring brass call. A beautifully shaped B theme forms around this "call". The important thematic material of the work can be found between measures 30 and 45:

Ex. 118

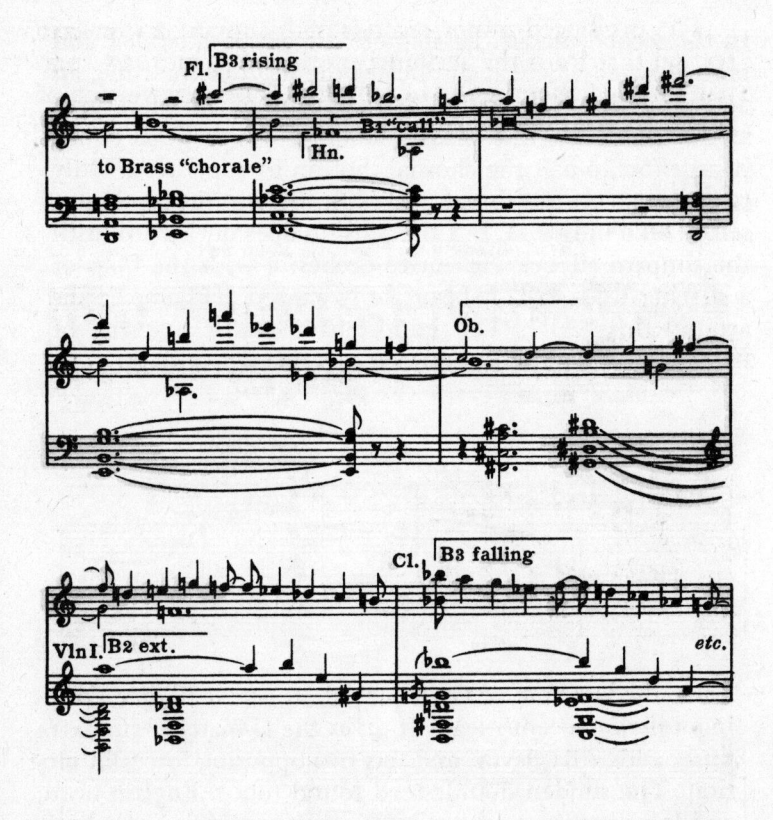

The diatonic tail of B1 promotes a chorale-like extension in the brass while the disjunct head of B1 grows contrapuntally sly (B3) as it coils around the "chorale", hiding its most characteristically melodic leaps. The brass extension consists solely of parallel minor triads, but these triads are used to color a single melodic line played against two free voices (from B2) in mixed strings and woodwinds. This fresh three-part contrapuntal idea is surprised by a unison declamation of pure B1 in four loud horns. The eighth notes in the strings then change to accelerating sixteenths and halt before the second large division of the dance.

The prolonged minor seconds of A support a capriccio section that leads the sustained motifs of A into fast company while flattening the humps of B. This new version of A and B forms the C material:

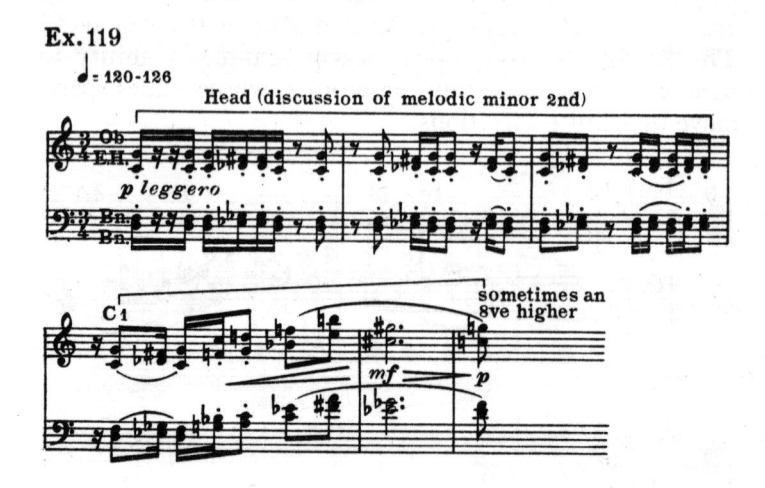

Ex. 119

Later the last note of C1 is played an octave higher, forming a major seventh leap. It gives the C material an extra push, adds a B1 flavor, and sets two opposing forces in motion. The sudden double-reed sound (oboe, English horn, and bassoons) is shocking and unnerves the first rhythmic phrase of this section. The jittery capriccio grows in excitement when a soothing motif fails to quiet it:

Ex. 120

Presently, C₁ and C₂ are spun into one line as miscellaneous B materials syncopate themselves contrapuntally around the line. C₁ noisily breaks in two as the brasses hammer the head of C₁ as they did with A, and the strings engage in a full harmonic development of the rest of C. This string harmony shows clearly Schuman's ability to handle shifting dissonant harmonies whose inner parts move in definite directions:

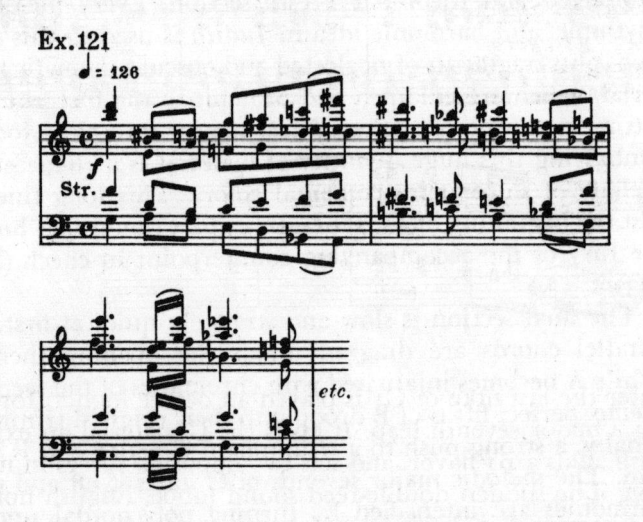

Ex. 121

The voices form intriguing folds in the harmonic structure. This type of harmony is used extensively in a later work, the Fourth String Quartet.

The section culminates on a rock-bottom C-sharp minor chord while the horns insist on making clear the new version of B₁—the "call" in pure perfect fifths with the tritone removed:

Ex. 122

A and B are jelled in the next quiet section as B3 occasionally falls melodically into the reassuring repeated chords of A. As echoes of C1's major seventh interval are heard, brash remarks from the capriccio chords of C discourage them and A settles comfortably on a soft-textured polychord while listening to a solo violin sing the perfect fifths of the B call.

The timpani pick out the perfect fifths and dive into a prolonged and turbulent Presto section. Every melodic, rhythmic, and harmonic idea in *Judith* is used in this section, plus fragments of neglected and obscure thematic material, which are enlarged and brought to the foreground, setting new aspects of the subject matter into clear focus. Embracing this huge quantity of material is a 46-measure melody of shifting instrumental colors. This long line is just the beginning of a gigantic three-part canon that holds the fury of the accompanying counterpoint in check (Ex. 123).

The final section is slow and strangely quiet at first, as parallel chords are dragged under the opening theme. While A becomes infatuated with chromatics of the second theme, perfect fifths of B droop into their original tritones. Finally, a strong push to a triumphant C-major end is begun. The melodic major seventh of C starts it off and the harmonies are intensified by turning polychordal under the melodic cadential figure of B2. As the pulse quickens, the brass state, in rich harmonic terms, the true *Judith* theme (ABC). And immediately the orchestra moves towards the final C-major cadence. It is not until the trumpet high A-flats are convinced that they cannot hold out against the C-E-G chord that a full and pure C-major sound is obtained. The timpani are struck rapidly with hard sticks (coda figure of Section I) causing the orchestra to vibrate with a tonic roar.

Ex. 123

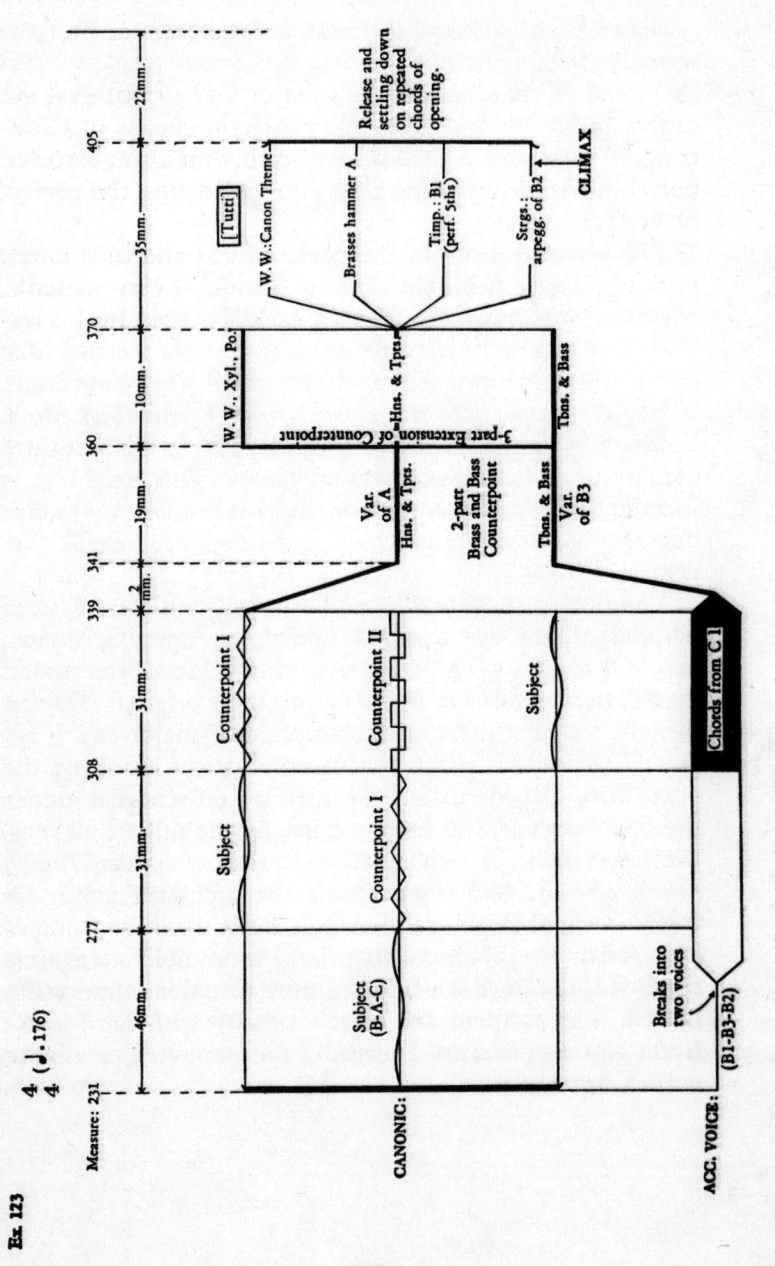

APPENDIX

I. List of Works

Title	Date of Completion	First Performance	Publisher
Four Canonic Choruses for Mixed Voices, a cappella	1932-33	May 3, 1935. A Cappella Choir, Teachers College, Columbia University, Carl Gutekunst, Dir.	G. Schirmer
1. *Epitaph* (Edna St. Vincent Millay)			
2. *Epitaph for Joseph Conrad* (Countee Cullen)			
3. *Night Stuff* (Carl Sandburg)			
4. *Come not* (Alfred Tennyson)			
*Canon and Fugue. For Violin, 'Cello, and Piano	1934		MS
*Choreographic Poem. For 7 instruments	1934		MS
*Symphony No. I. For 18 instruments	1935	Oct. 21, 1936. Gotham Sym. Orch. con. Jules Werner	MS
*String Quartet No. I	1936	Oct. 21, 1936. New String Quartet	MS
*Prelude and Fugue. For Orchestra	1937		MS
*Symphony No. II	1937	May 25, 1938. Greenwich Orch. con. Edgar Schenkman	MS
Pioneers! For 8-Part Chorus of Mixed Voices, a cappella (Walt Whitman)	1937	May 23, 1938. Westminster Festival Chorus con. Henry Switten	J. & W. Chester
Choral Etude. For Chorus of Mixed Voices, a cappella	1937	Mar. 16, 1938. Madrigal Singers con. Lehman Engel	C. Fischer
String Quartet No. II	1937	Spring, 1938. Forum String Quartet	Arrow Music Press

*Withdrawn pending revision.

Title	Date of Completion	First Performance	Publisher
Quartettino for Four Bassoons	1939	New Music Quarterly Recording	Boletín Latino-Americano de Música, 1941, Suplemento Musical
Prologue. For Chorus of Mixed Voices and Orch. (Genevieve Taggard)	1939	May 7, 1939. Federal Sym. Orch., Chorus of N. Y. High School of Music and Art, con. Alexander Richter	G. Schirmer
American Festival Overture	July 28, 1939	Oct. 6, 1939. Boston Sym. Orch. con. Koussevitzky	G. Schirmer
Prelude. For Chorus of Women's Voices, *a cappella* (Thomas Wolfe) [Also arr. for Mixed Voices, *a cappella*]	Nov. 1939	Apr. 24, 1940. Chorus of Sarah Lawrence Coll. con. Composer	G. Schirmer
String Quartet No. III	Dec. 1939	Feb. 27, 1940. Coolidge Quartet	G. Schirmer
This is Our Time. Secular Cantata No. 1, for Chorus of Mixed Voices and Orch. (Genevieve Taggard)	June 1940	July 4, 1940. People's Phil. Choral Soc., N. Y. Phil.Sym. Orch. con Smallens	Boosey & Hawkes
Symphony No. III	Jan. 11, 1941	Oct. 17, 1941. Boston Sym. Orch. con. Koussevitzky	G. Schirmer
Symphony No. IV	Aug. 17, 1941	Jan. 22, 1942. Cleveland Orch. con. Rodzinski	G. Schirmer
Newsreel. In Five Shots. For Band [Also arr. for orch.]	Nov. 16, 1941	1942. Pennsylvania State College Band, con. George S. Howard	G. Schirmer

Title	Date of Completion	First Performance	Publisher
Requiescat. For Chorus of Women's Voices and Piano [Also arr. for Mixed Voices and Piano]	Feb. 4, 1942	Apr. 4, 1942. Chorus of Sarah Lawrence Coll. con. Composer	G. Schirmer
Holiday Song. For Chorus of Mixed Voices and Piano (Genevieve Taggard) [Also arr. for Women's Voices and Piano]	May 26, 1942	Jan. 13, 1943. Collegiate Chorale con. Robert Shaw	G. Schirmer
Concerto for Piano and Small Orchestra	July 18, 1942	Jan. 13, 1943. Rosalyn Tureck, Saidenberg Sinfonietta con. Saidenberg	G. Schirmer
A Free Song. Secular Cantata No. 2, for Chorus of Mixed Voices and Orch. (Walt Whitman)	Oct. 16, 1942	Mar. 26, 1943. Harvard Glee Club, Radcliffe Choral Soc., Boston Sym. Orch. con. Koussevitzy	G. Schirmer
Prayer in Time of War. For Orchestra	Jan. 2, 1943	Feb. 13, 1943. Pittsburgh Sym. Orch. con. Reiner	G. Schirmer
Three-Score Set. For Piano	June 6, 1943	Aug. 29, 1943. Jacques de Menasce	G. Schirmer
Symphony for Strings	July 31, 1943	Nov. 12, 1943. Boston Sym. Orch. con. Koussevitzky	G. Schirmer
William Billings Overture	Nov. 26, 1943	Feb. 17, 1944. N. Y. Phil.-Sym. Orch. con. Rodzinski	G. Schirmer
Steeltown (Music for a film)	Feb. 1944	O.W.I. war film	MS
Variation on a Theme by Eugene Goossens. For Orch.	1944	Apr. 1945. Cincinnati Sym. Orch. con. Goossens	MS

Title	Date of Completion	First Performance	Publisher
Circus Overture (Side Show). For Orch.	July 20, 1944	Dec. 17, 1944. Schubert Theatre, Phila., con. Abravanel (small orch. version) Jan. 7, 1945. Pittsburgh Sym. Orch. con. Reiner (sym. orch. version)	G. Schirmer
Orpheus with his Lute. For Voice and Piano.	Aug. 6, 1944		G. Schirmer
Te Deum. (For the Coronation Scene of Shakespeare's *Henry VIII*). For Chorus of Mixed Voices, *a cappella*	Aug. 1944	Apr. 1945. Harvard Glee Club, Chorus of Sarah Lawrence Coll. con. Woodworth	G. Schirmer
Undertow (Choreographic Episodes for Orch.)	Feb. 22, 1945	Apr. 10, 1945. Ballet Theatre, N. Y. con. Dorati. Nov. 29, 1945. Los Angeles Phil. con. Wallenstein	G. Schirmer
Truth Shall Deliver (Geoffrey Chaucer, adapted by Marion Farquhar). For Chorus of Men's Voices *a cappella*	May 20, 1946	Dec. 7, 1946. Yale Glee Club, con. Bartholomew	G. Schirmer
Night Journey. Ballet	Apr. 9, 1947	Feb. 17, 1948. Martha Graham, Harvard Univ.	MS
Concerto for Violin and Orch.	July 13, 1947 (rev. 1954)	Feb. 10, 1950. Isaac Stern, Boston Sym. Orch. con. Munch	G. Schirmer
Symphony No. VI	Dec. 31, 1948	Feb. 27, 1949. Dallas Sym. Orch. con. Dorati	G. Schirmer

Title	Date of Completion	First Performance	Publisher
Judith (Choreographic Poem for Orch.)	Aug. 28, 1949	Jan. 4, 1950. Martha Graham, Louisville Orch. con. Robert Whitney	G. Schirmer
George Washington Bridge. For Band	Apr. 17, 1950	July 30, 1950. National Music Camp, Interlochen, Mich.	G. Schirmer
The Mighty Casey (Jeremy Gury). Opera	1951-53	May 4, 1953. Julius Hartt Musical Foundation, Hartford, Conn., staged by Elmer Nagy, con. Moshe Paranov	G. Schirmer
Voyage. A Cycle of Five Pieces for Piano.	Apr. 19, 1953	Aug. 18, 1953. Lillian Steuber, Chicago	Howard (G. Schirmer, agent)

II. List of Records

Works are listed in alphabetical order by title. The year given is the release date of the recording.

American Festival Overture
National Symphony Orchestra, conducted by Hans Kindler. 2 sides, 12" 78 rpm [1942]. RCA Victor 18511 (out of print).
Vienna Symphony Orchestra, conducted by Walter Hendl. 1/2 side, 12" 33 1/3 rpm [1953]. American Recording Society 115.
Note: The disc also contains Harris's Symphony No. 3 and Sessions's The Black Maskers.

Choral Etude
Madrigal Singers, conducted by Lehman Engel. 1 side, 10" 78 rpm [1939]. Columbia C-17139D (out of print).

George Washington Bridge
Eastman Wind Ensemble, conducted by Frederick Fennell. 1/3 side, 12" 33 1/3 rpm [1953]. Mercury MG 40006.
Note: the disc also contains band pieces by Bennett, Barber, Gould, Persichetti, and Piston.

Judith
Louisville Orchestra, conducted by Robert Whitney. 1 side, 12" 33 1/3 rpm. See *Undertow*, below.

String Quartet No. III
Gordon Quartet. 6 sides, 3 12" 78 rpm [1948]. Concert Hall AB.

String Quartet No. IV
Juilliard String Quartet. 1 side, 12" 33 1/3 rpm [1952]. Columbia ML 4493.
Note: the other side contains Ingolf Dahl's Concerto a tre.

Quartettino for Four Bassoons
[Information about the performers lacking]. 1 side, 12" 78 rpm [1939]. New Music Quarterly Recording (out of print).

Symphony for Strings
> Concert Hall Symphony Orchestra, conducted by **Edgar Schenkman**. 8 sides, 4 12" 78 rpm [1947, for subscribers only]. Concert Hall CH-A 11. Also 1 side, 12" 33 1/3 rpm [1951]. CHS 1078.
> Pittsburgh Symphony Orchestra, conducted by William Steinberg. I side, 33 1/3 rpm [1953]. Capitol S-8212.
> *Note: the other side contains Ernest Bloch's Concerto Grosso for String Orchestra and Piano.*

Symphony No. III
> Philadelphia Orchestra, conducted by Eugene Ormandy. 2 sides, 12" 33 1/3 rpm [1951]. Columbia ML 4413.

Symphony No. VI
> Philadelphia Orchestra, conducted by Eugene Ormandy. Columbia, in preparation.

Three-Score Set
> Andor Foldes, piano. 1 side, 10" 78 rpm, 16070, included in an album-set of 4 10" discs [1947]. Vox 174.
> *Note: The album is entitled* Contemporary American Piano Music *and also contains pieces by Bowles, Barber, Copland, Harris, Piston, Sessions, and Thomson.*

Undertow
> Louisville Orchestra, conducted by William Schuman. 1 side, 12" 33 1/3 rpm [1951]. Mercury MG 10088.
> *Note: The other side contains* Judith, *conducted by Whitney.*

III. Selected List of Articles by William Schuman

Listed in order of publication

A Novel One-Volume Encyclopedia, in Modern Music, Nov.-Dec. 1937, pp. 128-30. [Review of Slonimsky's *Music Since 1900.*]
Unconventional Case History, in Modern Music, May-June 1938, pp. 222-27.
Layman's Guide and Student Opera, in Modern Music, Jan.-Feb. 1939, pp. 135-37. [Reviews of Copland's *What to Listen for in Music* and *The Second Hurricane.*]
Taylor-Made Topics, in Modern Music, Mar.-Apr. 1940, pp. 197-99. [Review of Deems Taylor's *The Well-Tempered Listener.*]
Writing for Amateurs and Pros, in the New York Times, June 30, 1940, music section, p. 5. [Concerning *This is Our Time.*]
A Brief Study of Music Organizations Founded in the Interest of the Living Composer, in Twice a Year, V-VI (1940/41), 361-67.
Songs America Has Sung, in the New York Times, June 13, 1943, book review section, p. 8. [Review of *A Treasury of American Song* by Downes and Siegmeister.]
Music Master, in the New York Times, June 27, 1943, Book Review, p. 4. [Review of Burk's *The Life and Works of Beethoven.*]
A Symphonic Composer on Some Current Problems, in Music Publishers Journal, Sept.-Oct. 1943, pp. 5, 39.
The Final Triumph, in Minna Lederman, ed., Stravinsky in the Theatre, New York, 1948, pp. 134-35.
Virtuosity in Discernment, in Jerome Mellquist & Lucie Wiese, eds., Paul Rosenfeld, Voyager in the Arts, New York, 1948, pp. 105-08.
On Teaching the Literature and Materials of Music, in The Musical Quarterly, April 1948, pp. 155-68.
A Composer Looks at Critics, in Musical America, Nov. 15, 1948, pp. 8, 31.
On Freedom in Music, in Sculley Bradley, ed., *The Arts in Renewal*, Philadelphia, 1951, pp. 67-106.
The Side of the Angels, in Etude, June 1951, pp. 9f, 50.
Introduction, in *The Juilliard Report on Teaching the Literature and Materials of Music*, New York, 1953, pp. 7-24.
The Place of Composer Copland, in the New York Times, Nov. 8, 1953, book review section, pp. 3, 49.

IV. Selected Bibliography of Articles on and References to William Schuman

The entries are arranged alphabetically by author

Bernstein, Leonard. *The Latest from Boston,* in *Modern Music,* Mar.-Apr. 1939, p. 183. [Review of Schuman's Second Symphony.]
——— *Young American—William Schuman,* in *Modern Music,* Jan.-Feb. 1942, pp. 97-99.
Broder, Nathan. *The Music of William Schuman,* in *The Musical Quarterly,* Jan. 1945, pp. 17-28.
——— *Current Chronicle,* in *The Musical Quarterly,* Apr. 1950, pp. 279-82. [Review of the Violin Concerto.]
Copland, Aaron. *Current Chronicle,* in *The Musical Quarterly,* July 1951, pp. 394-96. [Review of String Quartet No. IV.]
Erskine, John. *My Life in Music,* New York, 1950, pp. 135, 254-58, 264.
Eyer, Ronald F. *William Schuman,* in *Musical America,* Jan. 25, 1944, pp. 8, 25.
Frankenstein, Alfred. *William Schuman,* in *Modern Music,* Nov.-Dec. 1944, pp. 23-29.'
Garoutte, Nancy. *Bill Schuman,* in *Sarah Lawrence Alumnae Magazine,* Fall 1944, pp. 14, 22.
Glock, William. *Music,* in The Observer (London), Sept. 2, 1945, p. 2. [Column devoted to Schuman's music.]
Goldman, Richard F. *Current Chronicle,* in *The Musical Quarterly,* Apr. 1951, pp. 254-60. [Review of *Judith*.]
Kiekhofer, William H. *To Thee, Wisconsin, State and University,* New York, 1950, p. 110. [Citation of Schuman for honorary degree.]
Persichetti, Vincent. *Current Chronicle,* in *The Musical Quarterly,* Apr. 1952, pp. 298-301. [Review of Symphony No. VI.]
Rosenfeld, Paul. *Current Chronicle,* in *The Musical Quarterly,* July 1939, pp. 379-81.
Schuman, William, in *Current Biography,* June 1942, pp. 66-67.
Thomson, Virgil. *The Art of Judging Music,* New York, 1948, pp. 157-59 [Schuman's *Undertow*] and 310-13 ["Theory" at Juilliard].

Index

Abravanel, Maurice, 22n
Academy of Arts and Letters, 26
Advisory Committee on American Music for Columbia Records, 45
American Society of Composers, Authors and Publishers, 18

Bach, Johann Sebastian, 29, 33
Ballet Theatre, 21, 108
Barber, Samuel, 86
Barlow, Howard, 17
Bartholomew, Marshall, 31
Bearns Prize, 14f
The Beggar's Opera (Britten), 31n
Benkard, Franklin B., 29
Benkard, Mrs. J. Philip, 26
Bennington College, 23
Berger, Arthur, 23
Bergsma, William, 31
Berlioz, Hector, 41, 44
Bernstein, Leonard, 17
Bloch, Ernest, 31n
Boosey and Hawkes, 43
Boston Daily Globe, 21
Boston Herald, 20, 21
Boston Symphony Orchestra, 17f, 19ff, 23
Boston Transcript, 18
Brant Lake Camp, 11
Broder, Nathan, 43

Carmen (Bizet), 41
Caruso, Enrico, 3
Charak, Amy, 18f
Charak, Walter, 19
Charman, Florida, 42
Chaucer, Geoffrey, 129
Chicago Symphony Orchestra, 27

Cleveland Orchestra, 20
Collegiate Chorale, 21
Columbia Broadcasting System, 17
Composers' Forum Laboratory, 15
Coolidge Quartet, 19
Copland, Aaron, 16f, 18, 86
Cullen, Countee, 14n, 126

Dallas Symphony League, 30, 47
La Damoiselle Elue (Debussy), 23
Dewey, John, 12
Downes, Olin, 19, 20f, 27
Dreiser, Theodore, 21
Drinker, Henry S., 29f
Dushkin, Samuel, 30

Elizabeth Sprague Coolidge Foundation, 30
Engel, Carl, 24ff, 30
Engel, Lehman, 16
Erskine, John, 28f, 32

Farquhar, Marion, 129
Fitzgerald, F. Scott, 6
Frankenstein, Alfred, 27

Gilbert, Francis, 26
The Girl of the Golden West (Puccini), 22
Glock, William, 27
Goethe, Johann Wolfgang von, 1
Goldman, Richard Franko, 31
Graham, Martha, 30, 114
Grasso, Benjamin, 42f
Greenwich Village Orchestra, 17
Grenell, Horace, 11
Group Theatre, 41
Guggenheim Fellowship, 26

Gury, Jeremy, 22, 130
Haggin, B. H., 28
Harris, Roy, 18f, 21, 27, 36, 67, 68, 84, 86
Hartt Music School, Hartford, 22
Harvard Glee Club, 23f
Harvard Symposium on Music Criticism, 30
Harvard University, 23
Haubiel, Charles, 9
Haydn, Franz Josef, 12
Heilbrunn, Louis (grandfather), 1f
Heinsheimer, Hans W., 43
Henry VIII (Shakespeare), 24, 129
Herbert, Victor, 3
Hillyer, Raphael, 31n
Hindemith, Paul, 31n
Hunter College, 4
Hutcheson, Ernest, 28, 29

Ibsen, Henrik, 41
Ives, Charles, 84

Johnson, Edward, 29, 30
Johnson, Thor, 31
Juilliard Quartet, 31n
Juilliard Report on Teaching the Literature and Materials of Music, 33f
Juilliard School of Music, 15, 28-35, 40, 41, 43, 44, 45, 47

Koff, Robert, 31n
Kolodin, Irving, 19
Koussevitzky Music Foundation, 21, 26, 45
Koussevitzky, Serge, 17f, 20, 23, 31n

Lauder, Sir Harry, 1f
League of Composers, 19, 26
Lloyd, Norman, 24, 31
Loesser, Frank, 6
Los Angeles Philharmonic Orchestra, 22

Louisville Philharmonic Society, 30, 114
Louisville, University of, 68n

Malkin Conservatory, 8f
Mann, Robert, 31n
Marks, Edward B., Jr., 5
Mason, Daniel Gregory, 14f
McCollester, Parker, 29
Mennin, Peter, 31
Metropolitan Opera Association, 26
Metropolitan Opera House, 21
Millay, Edna St. Vincent, 14n, 126
Modern Music, 16, 24, 27
Monteux, Pierre, 26f
Mozart, Wolfgang Amadeus, 41
The Musical Quarterly, 16, 18

Nauheim, Ferdinand, 10
Naumburg Musical Foundation, 42
The New Republic, 40
The New School for Social Research, 28
New Statesman and Nation, 40
New York Herald Tribune, 22, 23, 40
New York Philharmonic-Symphony Society, 7, 29n, 44
New York Times, 21, 40
New York University School of Commerce, 6, 8
The New Yorker, 20
Newsweek, 22

Oberly and Newell (printing firm), 2, 10
Oberon Overture (Weber), 4
Odets, Clifford, 41
Oedipus Rex (Stravinsky), 31n
Ormandy, Eugene, 20
Otello (Verdi), 41

Paramount Advertising Agency, 8
Parsifal (Wagner), 41

Pennsylvania State College, 23
People's Philharmonic Chorus, 19
Perry, John, 29
Persichetti, Vincent, 31
Persin, Max, 9, 42
Philadelphia Orchestra, 20
Prince, Frances (see Schuman, Frances)
Princeton University, 23
Pulitzer Prize, 26

Radcliffe Choral Society, 23
Rodzinski, Artur, 20
Roosevelt, Franklin Delano, 40
Rose, Billy, 22
Rosenfeld, Paul, 18, 27
Ross, Anthony, 5

Saidenberg Sinfonietta, 21
Sandburg, Carl, 14n, 126
Sarah Lawrence College, 11f, 14, 23f, 26, 28, 33, 42, 79
Schenkman, Edgar, 17
Schiller, Johann Christoph Friedrich von, 1
Schirmer, G., Inc., 24ff, 28, 30, 42f, 45
Schirmer, Gustave, 30
Schirmer, Mrs. Rudolph, 26
Schubart, Mark, 31
Schuhmann, Moritz (grandfather), 1f
Schuhmann, Rosa (grandmother), 1
Schuman, Andrea (daughter), 39
Schuman, Anthony William (son), 38f
Schuman, Audrey (sister), 3, 4, 7
Schuman, Frances (wife), 13, 14, 36, 38, 42
Schuman, Ray [i.e. Rachael] (mother), 1, 2, 3, 8
Schuman, Samuel (father), 1, 2, 3, 8f, 10
Schuman's works:
    A Free Song, Secular Cantata No. II, 23, 26, 27, 60, 63, 80, 82, 128
    American Festival Overture, 18f, 26, 27, 53, 86-92, 127, 131
    Canon and Fugue, 126
    Choral Etude, 52, 83, 126, 131
    Choreographic Poem, 14, 126
    Circus Overture (Side Show), 22, 67n, 129
    Come Not, No. 4 of Four Canonic Choruses, 14n, 126
    Concerto for Piano and Small Orchestra, 21, 59, 62, 63, 68f, 74, 128
    Concerto for Violin and Orchestra, 30, 55ff, 59, 60, 67n, 114
    Epitaph, No. 1 of Four Canonic Choruses, 14n, 82, 126
    Epitaph for Joseph Conrad, No. 2 of Four Canonic Choruses, 14n, 126
    Fair Enough, 11
    Fate, 5
    Four Canonic Choruses for Mixed Voices, 14n, 16, 24, 25, 51, 82, 126
    George Washington Bridge, 30, 130, 131
    Holiday Song, 25, 73, 128
    In Love with a Memory of You, 6
    It's Up to Pa, 5
    Judith, 30, 59, 68n, 84, 85, 114-123, 130, 131
    Newsreel. In Five Shots, 19n, 23, 73, 127
    Night Journey, 30, 39, 54, 67f, 114, 129
    Night Stuff, No. 3 of Four Canonic Choruses, 14n, 126
    Orpheus with his Lute, 24, 129
    Pioneers!, 16, 83, 126
    Prayer in Time of War (Prayer-1943), 25, 128

Prelude and Fugue, 126
Prelude for Voices, 23, 80, 127
Prologue, 18, 19, 24f, 81, 127
Quartettino for Four Bassoons, 53, 54, 127, 131
Requiescat, 25, 71, 128
Side Show (see *Circus Overture*)
Steeltown, 128
String Quartet No. I, 16, 126
String Quartet No. II, 18, 52, 53, 65, 70, 126
String Quartet No. III, 19, 26, 51, 53, 54, 67, 127, 131
String Quartet No. IV, 16, 30, 48, 50, 57, 58, 64, 74, 84, 85, 114, 121, 131
Symphony for Strings, 21, 27, 54, 55, 59, 66, 72, 103-108, 128, 132
Symphony No. I, 14ff, 84, 126
Symphony No. II, 16ff, 20, 72, 126
Symphony No. III, 20, 25ff, 53, 65, 69f, 74-78, 93-102, 127, 132
Symphony No. IV, 20f, 30, 65, 67, 79, 127
Symphony No. VI, 46, 47, 59, 74, 78, 84, 85, 114, 129, 132
Te Deum, 24, 63, 129
The Mighty Casey, 22f, 85, 130
This is Our Time, Secular Cantata No. I, 19f, 58, 127
Three-Score Set, 25, 59, 60, 128, 132
Truth Shall Deliver, 31, 64, 129
Undertow, 21f, 27, 61f, 78, 108-113, 129, 132
Variation on a Theme by Eugene Goossens, 128
Voyage, 84, 85, 130
William Billings Overture, 20n, 52, 128
Schumann, Robert, 7, 27, 44

Schwarz, Blanche, 3, 13
Sessions, Roger, 16, 42, 84, 86
Shaw, Robert, 21, 31, 79
Simon, Henry, 20
Smallens, Alexander, 19f
Smith, Moses, 18
Strauss, Richard, 76
Swinford, Jerome, 11

Taft, William Howard, 40
Taggard, Genevieve, 20, 80, 127, 128
Tchaikovsky, Peter Ilyitch, 108
Teachers College, Columbia University, 10f
Tennyson, Alfred, Lord, 14n, 126
Thomson, Virgil, 21, 22, 27, 86
Time, 30
Tudor, Antony, 21, 108
Tureck, Rosalyn, 21

UNESCO, 40
U. S. State Department, 40

Vassar College, 23
Vinci, Leonardo da, 10, 12

Wagenaar, Bernard, 16
Wagner, Richard, 7, 41
Wallenstein, Alfred, 22
Warburg, James, 28f
Warburg, Kay, 28
Ward, Robert, 31
Wardwell, Alice, 29
Waring, Fred, 21
Warren, Constance, 11, 12, 42
Webster, Margaret, 24
Werner, Jules, 15
Wertheim, Ruth (cousin), 3
Whitman, Walt, 3, 16, 23, 80, 126, 128
Whitney, Robert, 114
Wilder, Thornton, 40
Wilfred Publishing Company, 10
Williams College, 23

138

Winograd, Arthur, 31n
Wisconsin, University of, 35
Wolfe, Thomas, 23, 80, 127
Works Progress Administration, 13, 17

Yale Glee Club, 31
Yale University, 31